2.50

Rhythm in the Heavens

Dancing in the Temple of Belur, Mysore State

RAM GOPAL

Rhythm in the Heavens

AN AUTOBIOGRAPHY

London
SECKER AND WARBURG
1957

Printed in England
at The Windmill Press
and
first published in 1957
by
Martin Secker & Warburg Ltd
7 John Street, London,
W.C.1

© Rom Gopal, 1957

आाङ्किं भुवनं यस्य वाचिकं सर्ववाङ्मयम् ।
आहार्यं चन्द्रताराादि तं नुमः सात्विकं शिवम् ॥

"To Whom the Whole World is the movement of
His body, All Music is his Speech, Adorned with
the Jewels of the Moon and Stars in His hair, deep
in stilled meditation, To this Almight Being Siva,
I make my Obeisance"

★

"For the naked soul there is neither Occident nor
Orient. These are only the garments. The world
is his home. And his home, being of all, belongs
to all."—*Romain Rolland.*

CONTENTS

ILLUSTRATIONS

Prologue

M Y father once said to me: "Why do you dance?"
"I love to move, to leap, to float . . . well, just let
the spirit seize me at the sound of drums or music,"
I replied immediately. "You call it dancing, Father, I call it
rhythm."

That answer, given so long ago, in 'Torquay Castle', our
old colonial house in Bangalore, South India, still seems to
me the only valid reason for dancing. That my style of
dancing is Hindu, the oldest known surviving technique,
going back thousands of years, is perhaps not important; the
fact remains, however, that this wonderful technique helps
its disciples to express their emotions with great force, but
a force that is always held in control.

In this book, as in my dance, I am sharing something with
you, my audience and readers, and I hope that in this sharing
you will sense something of the rasas, or sentiments, as we
call them in India, of love, heroism, hatred, fear, disgust,
peace, and all the other facets that have influenced both the
good and the not so good in a life that ever reaches onward
and upward through the Dance. As I dance I now attempt to
write, and in writing, to create that first 'rhythm' that im-

pelled my feet and body and arms to rush wildly into a blinding thunderstorm and dance ecstatically and naked in that
dangerous thunderstorm on a Monsoon afternoon long, long
ago when I was a little boy. But of that episode more later.

During my travels I have been privileged to meet many of
the greatest personalities of the East and the West. Had I
not been a dancer, an artist, provoking the curiosity of a
public, would I have met so many of the great? I wonder.
There was Gandhi in my boyhood days in Bangalore, when he
vacationed in Nandi Hills outside Bangalore; Tagore, that
bearded, white sage of beauty and poetry; Ramana Maharishi
of Arunachala, the sage of the twentieth century, whom
millions of Hindus were lucky to have met; my dance Gurus,
Meenakshisundaram Pillai and Kunju Kurup. Many more of
the East also enriched my life in India, in Burma, Tibet and
the Himalayas. But above them all stands the love and influence of my parents, whom in India we regard as gods.
And quite rightly too, for they were godly in action, thought
and love towards their family.

And the West? I love the West. I am happy to be
'Westernised' as some Indians childishly accuse me. Of
course I am Westernised, bridging the gap between the East
and the West. I am gloriously Westernised. Being Westernised completes for me the circle of East and West and consequently gives me the added knowledge and harmony of being
a complete human being. What untold hours I have spent
contemplating works of art in the matchless museums and
galleries of Paris, London and New York, not to mention the
Hague, Amsterdam and the Scandinavian countries. Could
my guardian angels have chosen better instructors and
teachers than Michel Larionov and Gontcharova to tell me
first-hand of the glories of the ballet, décors, dancers, books,
and to take me to watch so many classes in the style and
technique of ballet in the classrooms of Kchesinska and Pre-

obrajenska and Volinine in Paris? And Mercedes De Acosta, of the burning eyes and pale face. Could I have found a more beautiful person and friend to initiate me into the mystery of the world of art and letters and their chosen personalities? Mercedes was to me a 'Lilac Fairy' from the *Sleeping Beauty*, bringing art into my life. She guided and formed so much in me who was ignorant of art and Life; I owe much to her. I met her at a party in the hilltop home of Bernadine Szold Fritz in Hollywood. From the outset I could not help feeling the power of her personal magnetism and I immediately came under the spell of her influence. Through her I came to realise our 'oneness with' humanity, instead of our 'separateness from' each other. The more readily mankind realises its 'oneness' the more quickly will the light shine within its heart. When that time finally comes, the "Supreme Intelligence which dances within the Soul" will reveal itself to us in that 'Rhythm in the Heavens' which we see above. I would like to quote from the essence of Ramana Maharishi's teaching, a passage which clarifies his philosophy in his own words:

"The body is insentient like an earthen pot, and to it there is not the 'I' sense. But we exist as the self-established *Atman*, even in deep sleep, where there is no body consciousness. Therefore 'I' is not the body. Who am 'I'? Whence am 'I'? In the hearts of those who, seeking thus with keen insight, stay in steadfast and tranquil abidance in the self, there shines forth God Realisation and Enlightenment, consciousness, self-luminous and perfect."

Here is an extract from a letter from another great sage, Sri Aurobindo, to a disciple:

"After all, for the greatest as for the smallest of us, our strength is not our own but given to us for the game that has to be played, the work that we have to do. The strength may be formed in us, but its present formation is not final—neither formation of power, nor formation of weakness. At any moment the formation may change—at any moment one sees, especially under the pressure of Yoga, weakness changing into power, the incapable becoming capable, suddenly or slowly the instrumental consciousness rising to a new stature or developing its latent powers. Above us, within us, around us is the All-Strength and it is that that we have to rely on for our work, our development, our transforming change. If we proceed with faith in the work, in our instrumentality for the work, in the power that missions us, then in the very act of trial, of facing and surmounting difficulties and failures, the strength will come, and we shall find our capacity to contain as much as we need of the All-Strength of which we grow more and more perfect vessels."

Here both Sri Aurobindo and Ramana Maharishi touch the dynamic 'activity' of Yoga, and not the 'escapist' refuge that so many in India and elsewhere believe the teachings of Yoga to be. It is Activity, stemming from a constructive contemplation and 'communion', that these great Masters, like those before them, found. And it is that which has constantly carried me forward through so many storms on the oft-times dark seas of life. If only more people could realise the strength and activating dynamism of Yoga, how much better equipped would they be to look failure, death and disappointment, in the face, and overcome these forces by inner realisation of the 'Absolute Truth' these masters found.

CHAPTER ONE

I Saw a God Dance

IT is one of those warm yet pallid Indian afternoons. There
is a strange stillness everywhere. A dry leaf scrapes
sleepily across the parched earth. The sky is changing
from its vivid morning blue to a grey coat of afternoon misti-
ness, a sort of diffused lighting and there is that, for me,
maddeningly exciting smell of distant wet earth. The winds
carry this smell so quickly and it comes upon me with re-
freshing expectancy—a combination of musk and *kus-kus*,
mingled with green grass and warm steam, floating on the
wind from the rain beating down a few miles away in the
fields and hills near where my home was. But my nostrils
look for more of that wonderful nature-fresh perfume, and
more of it is carried on the winds that now blow at more
frequent intervals.

My mother's garden looks from time to time like a still
water-colour fresco suspended over the earth, unreal. What
a profusion of colour, yellow and red hibiscus, honeysuckle,
flame of the forest *Gold Mohur*, that wonderful tree of fire-red
blossoms and grey bark, like smoke. The lawns lie like jade,
and lizards run from corner to corner; the four wonderful
silver oaks seem to sigh, their trunks strongly rooted, their

1

tops swaying from side to side and I catch a glimpse of silver leaves, against this glow that the sky seems to give to everything. Far away I hear a rumble of thunder, distant, threatening and yet for me somehow promising. My blood tingles. I know it is going to rain, for it is the beginning of the monsoons. So at last I can escape from the guardianship of the servants. My stern and ever-watchful father is asleep taking his afternoon siesta; and my mother rests in her rooms after the busy activities of house and garden.

I am free, or think I am. Everybody, everything seems strangely quiet. A squirrel scurries across the jade green lawns, a train rumbles past. I move silently, too afraid to upset the storm gods, silently dreading, and yet fearfully, joyfully expecting a wonderful cannon ball thunderclap to send my blood reeling and give me the great thrill that thunderstorms have always given me, sending an inexplicable sensation of rhythm and movement that make my body feel like bursting unless I tear off my clothes and run into the very midst of that storm and become one with it.

How often that had happened in the past. And here are the same strange symptoms of another storm, only I hope it will be more violent and more elemental and that the thunder claps will grow wilder and more frequent, and those great lightning flashes will last a little longer, for I always knew they were followed by the most tremendous thunder claps. Yes, that instinct of mine is right. I look up, the sky is darkening and my worst hopes are to be confirmed, there is going to be a very heavy cloudburst. Far away I can hear herdsmen driving the cattle and goats quickly to the nearest shelter they can find. Now the tall silver oaks give warning that the winds are getting stronger, for I see how their silver tops blow and bend, the fringe of neem and banyan trees skirting our garden walls move and sway violently, I see a shower of rose petals fall from an arbour off the greenhouse.

My God, let it rain, fiercely, violently; let there be thunder and lightning, and let there be those wonderful rivers of muddy red earth making little lakes and streams all over our garden.

"*Sono baba, Sono baba*, where are you? Papa will be angry, you are not resting and reading your books. Please get back to your rest and books in your room." . . . I hear the familiar cry of Gulab, the grand old Rajput valet-friend-servant of the family. I do the obvious; I climb up a small tree, laden with fruit and thick protective leaves, a jack fruit tree. Gulab will not look there for me. He is bound to go and look in the pigeon-house or the poultry farm at the rear of the house, for that is where he has usually found me before. I must hide this time, for I do not want to miss this storm and I know it is going to scare me to death and frighten me into a veritable ecstasy. I don't answer, and I see Gulab walk away and around the bend of the large old house. The wind blows faster, I rock in my hide-out. One of the older garden squirrels brushes past me as he, too, perhaps seeks shelter; I am still, quiet, motionless. He turns and looks at me, his large eyes enquiring and his tail still; he moves on up and is lost in the tree. I feel something rough and slight on my leg. It is one of those large lizards, garden variety, on my right foot; he looks like one of the prehistoric monsters I have seen in the 'Books of Knowledge' from father's library and I feel like letting out a yell, but then Gulab or the gardener may hear and I will have to go inside and rest in bed and read a silly book.

The lizard to my great relief, moves off my leg, looks over his sharp fins like a miniature crocodile and disappears. One of my sisters comes out of the house towards the tree, following that path in the garden. I catch a glimpse of her and pray she will not seek me out. She calls out to the gardener and passes right under the low hanging branches on which I am perched like one of those slender monkeys I see in the *Lal Bagh* zoo. Thank God she's moved off! But our dog, Lassie, follows her, sniffs around the bark of the tree and then looks up. She spies me and, being the sport she is, wags her tail and tells me she won't tell, and without barking, walks off in the wake of my sister. Looking up I get one fresh drop of rain right into my eye. Quickly the raindrops follow one another on the large green leaves of the jack tree above my head, sounding like a lot of little elves and birds scurrying on the roof-top of the trees. It is rain! The air now is thick with the incense of the grass and the earth and the strange odour of steam mingled with the sticky perfume of trees and flowers. Nobody can possibly come out of the house now, they wouldn't want to get wet. I must bathe in that rain and feel one with the trees and birds and flowers. I start to un-dress: off come my shirt and pants, I hide them, or try to, from the rain which is now coming down in sheets, amidst the largest leaves I can find in the rush of the storm.

Without a moment's warning there is the most blinding flash of lightning, followed ominously by a thunder clap so loud that the tree shakes. I remember stories vaguely told of the danger of being under a tree in the rain and of people being struck dead; in any case I feel so suddenly cold and frightened that I slip down, or fall off the low hanging branches and decide to make a dash for the portico. It is too late, again the lightning flashes, again the thunder roars. The rain is now a curtain of pure blinding crystal so that I can hardly see the old house.

Suddenly I feel warm, my feet itch and my body seems vitalised by some shock that touches within me some long-forgotten secret. I paddle madly in the little streams and wave my arms around, wildly delighted and happy. I seem to be possessed by some tremendous spirit and I cannot direct my own body or my own will into anything. I don't want to anyway. I just tremble in glorious freedom and happiness to be alone, all alone in this wild and glorious storm. I catch far away, a vague glimpse of the top of the trees swaying violently, agitated and dancing, bending and touching each other, it seems to me, up in the clouds. There is mud and slush, fresh-smelling earth carrying leaves and petals of hibiscus and rose at my feet, and there is curtain after curtain of silver sheeted rain pouring with all God's might and glory on the parched, quiet, patient earth, and I am naked and happy and dancing, wildly happy and at one with some great force I feel, but do not seek to understand.

I stamp, jump, roll in the water and the mud, rise and am instantly cleansed; and then move around walking and running happily. And right in the midst of this wild cavorting I suddenly glance up at the sky. The large drops of rain beat into my eyes and make them smart, but this lasts only a second and I look up again and see in the blackness another flash, brighter than the last, hear an even more violent thunder clap, and suddenly remember what the Sanskrit professor working with my father every morning tells me. "When you see the lightning flash and hear the thunder drums up in the clouds and it rains, it is the God Siva dancing his *Tandava*, his dance of creation. If you look carefully you will see Indra riding his great white elephant Iravata, bearing the thunderbolt in his hands; everything in nature is God, look and you will see."

These thoughts of the words of the Sanskrit professor, a Brahmin scholar working with my father, come to my mind in a flash. Nothing matters now, for I am free and alone. Far up in the sky right in the midst of everything, I am caught up in this wild primordial dance of Nature, of Siva, of God himself, and in the wake of this rain and thunder and wind I am transfigured. Some force has entered within me to be forever hidden within my innermost depths. This I know, this I feel,

B

but cannot quite understand or explain to myself. But I don't bother. I feel a great surge of wild energy and I feel the God-surge within me, through me, with me in this rhapsody of rain and earth and green and thunderous noise, this madly whirling dance of nature in her monsoon mood.

Suddenly I hear a shout: "*Sono baba* come inside at once, your father is getting up." It is Gulab again. How I hate the thought of leaving all that wonderful fresh crystal clear bath of God and Nature, but how much more I fear looking into the angry eyes of my father and hear his deep voice reprove me for having risked catching cold! Impelled by fear of my father I slowly walk, start to go towards the great verandah; even the rain seems to have simmered down to less fury; as I walk, I catch the glint of sunlight coming quickly in patches and slipping off the leaves with the water into the wet red garden earth like silver. Unexpectedly I feel a rough grab on my shoulders. It is Gulab, who shakes me quickly out of my day-dreams. "If I tell Papa you know what will happen: you will get the cane, and you will cry and you will be made to stand for one hour in a solitary corner. You know that when Father gets up from his sleep every afternoon he is seldom in a good mood. Yet, *Sono Baba*, you never listen to me, not even if I warn you that you catch a bad cold and perhaps get very sick. Why?" I resent this chiding. "But Gullie," my nickname for him, "I will not get sick. Why should I get sick? The plants and birds and flowers and trees are cleaner, fresher, with the rain and they don't get sick and I don't believe that I will either. Besides, I shall save you bathing me this evening, for I am much cleaner now than I could be after going for my evening bath under the shower in the bath-room. Rainwater is warmer, but in there in the bathroom it's colder, even if it is hot, which you tell me it is, but it makes me shiver."

I look at him and I think he sees the sulky look in my eyes

and knows that any more talk of my harmless escapade will
only reduce me to tears and a moodiness that he knows well,
for he and the other servants complain that I am very like a
bull: hard, stubborn and impossible to handle once the mood
is upon me. Anyway, he says nothing more. I am quickly
led into the bathroom and scrubbed dry with a towel, new
clothes are brought and I am dressed up. I hear my mother
wake, her maids attending to her, bringing her a pot of
specially made coffee, and get an aroma that awakens my
appetite. I find myself hungry. My sullen mood vanishes,
now I want to eat, and to drink coffee with Mother. With an
admonishing finger from Gulab, I scamper out of the bath-
room, dry and shining, and run through the two rooms to
my mother's boudoir. She greets me with a warm hug and a
kiss. "Hey, child," she says, "your skin is so soft and fresh—
and," with a twinkle in her eyes, "cold. You wicked child,
out in the rain I suppose, bathing again! I heard thunder and
the maids shut the windows for fear of rain splashing on to
my bed. Tell me, was it a heavy fall?" "Yes, Mother,
wonderful, wonderful, and I danced naked." A deep sigh
from her. "I tell you it's dangerous, you may catch a cold,
don't you know? And you didn't stand under a tree, did you,
darling?" "No, Mother, not *under*; I was hiding in its
branches for a while, then I got scared, ran down the tree
and then changed my mind and decided to stay on and then
. . . well I just danced in the rain and I feel so fresh and
much, much cleaner than when Gullie baths me."

My mother looks at me long and lovingly, between sips of
her coffee. Perhaps the taste of that coffee and a recollection
of her own childhood, softens her reproaches towards me.
She looks at me, one of those sidelong glances coming out
from her wonderful face—a glance that is filled with laughter
and humour. She smiles and then laughs. "Come on, you
little devil, drink some coffee, only for goodness sake don't

let your father know; he'll say I am encouraging you to catch a cold, and, instead of you, the real culprit, getting a scolding, I shall be the one to get the full weight of his anger and——"

Suddenly, silently my father creeps in, like a Rajput panther in soft rubber-soled slippers. I always thought he wore them to enable him to move around noiselessly so that none of us could hear him and this would give him a sort of omnipresence in all the rooms of that big house. "You've had your bath early, Bisano, your hair looks damp. Why don't you dry properly?" I daren't trust my eyes to meet his. "Oh yes, Father, yes, I had a good bath and I'm drinking some coffee; my hair, oh yes, I'll dry it; it is almost dry, honestly, Father, Gulab rubbed it dry, see, feel." I move closer to him. "All right, son, run along and play now, but not outside in the wet garden; play inside on the floor of the verandah, and remember, not too much noise; now go on, run along."

I gulp my coffee, and my mother and I look at each other and I feel guilty and yet happily sly, for in our glances, unnoticed by my father, we've both had a joke at his expense, harmless and without a word spoken, but Father doesn't know what made both our eyes share, in that second, a laugh!

I peep out of a window. As suddenly as it started to get misty in the afternoon before the rain fell, it is now sunny, warm, blue. How quickly the earth is drinking up the water from heaven! It is almost dry again, not quite, but very nearly. And I think: 'Perhaps the earth likes to drink water as I do, after playing games in the hot sun, only the earth drinks more than I, or all of us children ever could in a whole year, in one afternoon's rainfall.'

Stepping out on to the verandah I see the little birds, all varieties, shiver and shake the water out of their feathers, stretching their legs, preening with their delicate beaks the wet feathers. And I wonder, did they enjoy it as much as I did? I am sure they did, for their eyes seem clear and bright, and I feel they are happy. Neighbouring children come to play, climbing over walls instead of using the road and coming up the drive to our house. Jumping walls being a quick way of saving precious hours for playing, it had become an un-written law that for play we jumped walls, for studies we walked the longest distance, to kill time! Then there was the gold and red curtain of sunset, swift and quick, and the red setting sun; soon it was night, and the cold, distant and yet bright stars all came out. Then dinner and bed. Tucking me in bed that night, Gulab didn't speak a word. I could see he was still afraid of what might have happened to him if Father caught me bathing in the rain, and before he switched out the light all he did was wave a threatening finger at me as much as to say: "If I catch you next time . . ." I fell asleep.

Looking back upon the gossamer tapestry of my childhood, how clearly I see certain pictures. The first pictures are those of the beauty of my home. And simultaneously I think of my mother and how much she meant to me and how much I loved her and how great was the influence of her love on my young life. Of course all children, everywhere, should think their parents are wonderful, but in India we are taught that one's parents are the earthly aspects of divinity upon earth; they stand on earth for the gods up in heaven, and we should touch their feet in reverence on special occasions, and always get their blessings at every opportunity.

You see my mother was Burmese, a Karen. And these folk, coming from the land of Burma, are often called the Irish of the East. Only there is more sun shining in Burma than ever shines in Ireland for all its magic, and the sad and grey churches of Ireland do not gleam like the rising, tower-ing, gold pagodas of my mother's country. Burma is a land of sunny people, smiling, quick tempered, hospitable and fun-loving, where the women work harder than the men. I was always proud of my mother when I used to walk with her in Bassein or Rangoon where I went with my parents on those few occasions as a child when they took me for my mother's annual visit to her native land.

How well I remember her. The walk of Burmese women is, I think, the most graceful, dignified and beautiful of any women anywhere in this world today, except perhaps those of Bali. And my mother walked like none other that I can remember from those far off childhood days. I recall the day she took me to visit the *Shwe Da Goan* pagoda in Rangoon. Her face, usually smiling, took on a distant, serious, meditative look. We went in a horse-drawn carriage. The coachman opened the door to us. My mother got out and then helped me out; I couldn't make the big distance to climb out of those high carriages without Mother literally carrying me down from the perched body that was the carriage. Then I remember she spread her Burmese parasol, a wonderful shell-pink affair with large painted chrysanthemums, over us, and we walked slowly and steadily up and up those never-ending steps to reach the main courtyard and temple of these fabulous shrines. On the way up we met innumerable poor people asking for alms. But I had eyes only for my mother. I remember tugging at her hand and begging her to allow me to buy some marigold and pink lotus and jasmine blossoms. They looked so beautiful and smelt so good, reminding me of our garden in Bangalore. And then after she had got them for me and when the time came for me to place them before the altar of Lord Buddha, I didn't want to part with them, and it was only after being scolded and made to feel ashamed by Mother that I hesitantly placed them on the altar of the reclining Buddha.

I was always so possessive of the beautiful. I resented anything, everything, that parted me from what my mind found beautiful and pleasing in nature and in life. I couldn't bear the night blotting out the sunset, or being made to leave lakes and the sea by my appointed wards. For it was like going back to darkness away from the beauty one drank of. My mother made me kneel at several shrines and burn incense sticks. How alluring is the perfume and smell of our Eastern Temples, be they Buddhist or Hindu. And what colourful places wherein to worship God. Surely God was a wonderful being full of colour and a love of ritual and beauty. How tenderly my mother explained to me the teaching of the Lord Buddha during those treasured visits to the pagoda, whether in Rangoon where our boat from India landed, or in the interior, sailing up the Irrawady river on our way to Bassein, the home of my parents before I was born in India.

My father settled in Bangalore, India, because the climate was so good and Bassein, he found, irritated what was liverish in his particular constitution. I was fortunate in that choice, for I was the richer for having drunk deep from the twin lands of Burma and India. And, as my mother used to say, both Burma and India were the richer and the more fortunate for having had Lord Buddha simplify in his eight-fold path the teachings of the ancient books and truths.

I can never forget the indelible impression it made on my mind and spirit, as my mother told me, from time to time the various stories of Jatakas of Lord Buddha and his spirit of love and sacrifice made in innumerable forms and incarnations before he, Lord Buddha, was reincarnated as the saviour of the world, and my mother told me this was all five hundred years before Jesus Christ came to enlighten Israel. "You see, darling, two of the world's great saviours of mankind were from the east; they rose like the sun which rises in the east. And you must try to believe and become one with the spirit of these God men, and this you can do if you listen carefully and read when you grow up all their preachings and stories and truths from the sacred books of those times. You see the Bible and the Dhammapada (book of Lord Buddha's teachings) are one."

"But tell me, Mother," I asked, "why does Lord Buddha lie down on his right side, and why does he wear gold robes, and why does he seem so calm and smiling? Shouldn't he look worried from telling everybody what to do and how to act in the right way? And why do all the pictures and statues of Christ show him bleeding with thorns in his head and nails in his hands? And why do the pictures and paintings I see in the Roman Catholic chapel and school always represent such terrible sufferings?" These were the recurring questions my dear mother was patiently made to answer from time to time. And she was always simple, direct, childlike in her answers to me about these perplexing questions that I, her young and quenchlessly eager son, kept asking her. And I preferred to ask her rather than Father. You see, my father had been put right off religion by a very strict grandfather. My father's grandfather, according to my father, used to rise at three in the morning and take a bath, winter or summer. The winters are bitingly cold in Ajmer and Bikaneer in Rajputana where my father was brought up. After bathing at this ungodly hour of the night, my father's grandpa, eager to enlighten his family would awaken his children and grandchildren and eagerly make them sit through the interminable *Pujas* (prayer ceremonies) in which all strict Hindus delight. Well, it may have taught the old gentleman a lot about God, but it completely put my father against the ritual and complicated system of worship. My father always said there was Truth, there was Nature, and there was one's Will, and if these were what God gave one, that was sufficient. But he believed that idol worship was a waste of time. Instead, he said, it was more useful to study and work and rely upon oneself. That was nearer Truth and the reason why we were born, and the way to achieve success.

So you see, my father's explanation of religion or philosophy to my thirsty mind did not illuminate me as did the method sought by my mother of colourfully and patiently explaining the mysteries of Lord Buddha. "One must love, one must be tolerant." Her slanting eyes looked more Buddha-like than ever as she explained it to me. "You see, Lord Buddha himself had gone through torments such as few can withstand; it was all the more difficult for him because he was born richer than the richest Indian Raja of today, and renounced it all. Imagine anybody asking you for your little toy engines, or your tops or kites that you treasure, how would you feel, giving them up? Well, Lord Buddha when he was Prince Siddhartha gave it up. From untold years of seeking, suffering and wanderings, the Truth finally dawned on him. And when he realised that great enlightenment, which you've seen depicted on the Buddhist temples painted in colourful frescoes, he gave richly, generously from his knowledge till the day he died and because it is Truth and from God, that giving and that light shine and enlighten the path of those who are tormented in the darkness of their own confused lives."

My mother's voice dropped to a whisper. I was ready to start crying because of the sadness with which my mother had told me the story; it was all so touching and so convincing and true. "But, Mother, everybody wants to be happy, why isn't everybody happy all the time, always?" I asked impatiently. My mother looked at me again and I thought somehow that her look reminded me of the reclining Buddha and his benign glance, filled with compassion and love. "But, my child, Lord Buddha's path and teachings unfold the greatest, most undreamed of happiness in this world. He who follows his teachings becomes the happiest person on earth. Don't you want to be happy, my son?"

"Yes, Mother, always happy, nothing but happy, but how?"

"Lord Buddha said that anyone who would weed out from his mind and heart all hatred and evil thoughts and all bad desires, and replace them with good thoughts and worthy desires, and fill his heart with charity towards others, and compassion towards suffering people and animals and life in general, while cultivating a sense of detachment from all worldly possessions, then that person awakens the Divinity within the spirit and within the self. And only then would the greatest peace and happiness follow simultaneously, instantly."

"Really, Mother?" I said. "Is that true? Then may I give away to him who asks, whatever he wants?" I clutched my mother's arm asking her this, impatiently waiting for a reply.

"Well, yes, my son, it is by giving that one pleases God."

CHAPTER TWO

Debut

"HIS HIGHNESS the Yuvaraja of Mysore has heard that you have some talent as a dancer, and wants you to appear this evening and dance at the Lalita Mahal. There will be a few people—about a thousand or so. It is very intimate and private. I believe the Viceroy will be there too. He is flying from Delhi to the special Durbar that the Maharaja, the brother of the Yuvaraja is attending. It is going to be a very special night. Besides, according to the astrologers, tonight the night of the New Moon, the time is Auspicious and the omens are good." It is my friend Devarajurs Speskin of the Royal House of Mysore speaking.

'His Highness wants me to dance,' I mused to myself, thinking slowly. My heart nearly burst at the very thought of dancing. A small party—just about a thousand 'intimate' guests! What could I wear? No head-dress, no jewels, nothing really. And for music? So went the ever-increasing circle of my thoughts, causing my head to reel with giddy anticipation. But I would do it. It was a challenge. It did not matter how—but I would try, and if the worst happened I could at least have fallen flat on my face and even that would be excused, for no one would say I was cowardly and that I lacked the courage to try?

Later that afternoon I asked my friend Devarajurs how would I, how could I dance? Did he realise my pathetic costumes and head-dresses and bells were hundreds of miles away in Bangalore? "Don't worry, Ram," he said. He picked up a telephone and rang the Palace, that great big myriad-lighted, garlic-domed and onion-roofed building with a million lights. "We are coming now. Yes . . . some jewels, pearls, emeralds and rubies, also some of the golden head-dresses that are placed on the Palace gods on festive days . . . yes . . ." Here he cupped his hand over the phone and turning to me, said: "You'll be ready to go right away, won't you? You can select the things you want to wear from the treasure-room." All this quite casually. Then into the phone again to the Palace: "Yes, we'll be along in half an hour." Silence. Not even a raised eyebrow. Just like that. The 'things'? What were these 'things' anyway? I could not dream it possible. But I did hear what he had said. And he was a man of his word.

We were driving down the beautifully lit avenues and laid out flowered gardens. We passed gaily lit fountains illuminated with concealed electric lights as their sprays shot up amid the flower-bedecked squares, and far away, hanging in the backdrop of all this was the pearl necklace of lights that covered the Chamundi Hill. But somehow everything blurred in my mind. "Watch out, there's a villager in the way . . . a child. . . ." There was a loud screeching of brakes, a hideous swerve. It is over now I thought, something terrible has happened. Either we are in a ditch or someone is killed. The car stood dead still. The driver, all turbaned and liveried, shot out and rushed to the back of the car. I opened my eyes. The strain was too much for me . . . my thoughts were already working me up into a frenzy of excitement and here, this wretched, awful accident had happened. And surely someone lay crushed, dead, mutilated behind that car. My nerves were strained to bursting. My friend Devarajurs had jumped out of the car. I turned round and gazed out of the back. And there, grinning sheepishly, was a villager, his child and a white cow. The driver was using rather heady language in that dialect, but I could see that made the peasant laugh more, as the little child clung to his legs, and my friend the regal and blue blooded Devarajurs, maintaining the dignity of the Royal House, surveyed with an affected calm the whole scene.

The cow was not amused. It just kept swishing its tail to drive away the annoying flies. Its jaws chewed some invisible grass and the big bell tied around its neck jingle-jangled as if it were walking through some quiet mountain glade! This was too much. I dashed out of the car and rushed out to my friend, shouting: "Go on, teach him a lesson . . . he'll kill himself next time. The cow is sacred, but he must learn road sense. There is that little child with him, but he stands like a blithering idiot, laughing. . . ." Before anyone could stop me I leapt at the bamboo stick the man was holding and severely belaboured him. "Now tell him" I said to the chauffeur, "he must remember that the life of a baby and his own are as sacred as that of this cow." To my exasperation, this had induced an even greater sense of amusement in the peasant's face. He laughed at me without any malice or anger that I had whipped him. The child cried. The cow chewed away at its invisible grass.

"Come on, Ram, we are already late for the treasure-room." We returned to the car and sped into the enormous arches of the Palace. Dazed and angered, my heart beat fast with excitement. It was only another two hours before I was to dance, and there we were casually mounting the heavily carpeted stairs of the Palace as if we had just driven through the gardens. And there had nearly been a terrible accident.

Now before me, as the doors swung open, lay the jewel-room. How can I describe it? Laid out in a profusion of shapes, sizes and colours was every conceivable kind of necklace, ring, anklet, ear-ring, head jewel and armlet that you could imagine. Under the naked and harsh electric lights they all invited me to wear them. Each jewel seemed to cry out to me to take it for the forthcoming dance. But I went for the most beautiful coloured gems. I chose some walnut-sized emeralds that looked like bits of frozen deep sea water, blood-red rubies the size of grapes and masses of pearls. Also, some of the beautifully enamelled necklaces. "You will look like the Tanjore Ikons of the Boy God Krishna—only you won't steal the butter, you'll steal the hearts of all those who watch you dance tonight," Devarajurs exclaimed. I was too excited to answer.

My cheeks were burning hot now. I was so little. Barely a boy. This was too much. I remember an hour later wearing and wrapping round my loins some gold and white silk cloth, tightly. I remember somebody anointing my body with sandal paste. And then the sudden shock my body got when those fabulous jewels touched my warm flesh. They were cold. They made me shiver. But truly they were wonderful to look at! Looking into a mirror, I could see them take on a new life. It seemed that for me the air was electric with something unusual that was about to take place. "Please, Devraj, give me something to sip, I am parched. Water, lemon, anything, but quick!" I gasped. I was about to go on. The first notes had struck. "Here, take this ivory stuff. It's not whisky or brandy, it's from apples and it's more bubble than alcohol," and he handed me a crystal-cut glass that looked like a jewelled half-open lotus flower. Without a thought and in complete trust at what he said, I took one long, deep draught of the stuff. For a few moments I felt nothing. Then my head began to see stars. Were these great chandeliers hanging above me or were they real stars?

My feet were like a winged eagle. I felt the contact of my soles on the wooden floor. Something within the pit of my stomach began to palpitate. And I thought that was how the big engines that I saw hissing along the rail tracks must feel . . . that is, if they could feel at all. My feet itched as though they were electric. There was that big Indian orchestra playing an Indian melody, and there I was spinning wildly dancing as Siva, God of the Stars and the Moon. And believe me—I have never felt so near the stars as I did then; I was actually dancing with them! I plucked the Crescent moon, wore that in my hair and made the most violent and passionate embraces to a big-bosomed invisible Goddess called Parvati, the Wife of Siva, in this mimed dance of mine. I felt all fire. My body bent, swayed, leapt and moved around that room like some piece of golden silk blown by the winds. And then I stopped.

For a few moments there was an ominous silence. My God, did they not like my dance? It was no good? I knew it, I did not have my usual costume and the Royal Family had seen their priceless jewels and were angry? Suddenly, like some deafening thunder clap the applause started from the raised dias where the Royal Ones were seated, and as if taking their cue from them the 'small intimate party' of a thousand or more guests started clapping, shouting and stamping on that enormous sprung wooden ballroom floor. I remember now, one of the drummers of the orchestra, seizing a stick and lashing at a drum in a frenzy of applause and excitement. I bowed. Sweat pouring from my body, I was led away by Devarajurs. His arm possessively held my hands, squeezing them till I felt one of the dragon rings studded with rubies bite into my fingers.

That 'bubbly' stuff which was neither brandy nor whisky, was something I had never drunk before. It was called champagne. It gave wings to my feet and gave me courage and

spirits I never knew existed within me. And it certainly
served the occasion in giving me that extra 'something' to
dance the way people later told me I did. They said I was
'possessed'. In India, when someone does something very,
very extraordinary to music or drums in the presence of a
crowd, it is often called 'possession'. It is either a Rakshasa
—a devil, or very rarely a Deva—an angel. In other words it
was either a devil or an angel. It was an angel that possessed
me, so I was told. I could not have cared less! But again it
was that same feeling, though different in a way, as that
'dancing in the rain' that had seized me in that thunderstorm,
only that dance seemed a long way away from this dance. I
was naked in that one, whereas now I did have a few emeralds
and rubies to cover me besides the loin cloth of white gold
and silk.

"Come, Ram, the Royal Ones want to see you. They are
pleased with you. Very pleased. Don't forget, address them
as 'Yes, your Highness'." Again I was led away, dressed in a
large scarlet shawl. "Remarkable performance, Ram Gopal
. . . my brother tells me you are hoping to revive the male
forms of temple dancing. Very good." How kindly the great
Maharaja looked, his eyes brimming with laughter in a mouth
that pursed itself shut with control. "You're a genius!
Wonderful! I've never seen anything like that dancing either
here in Mysore or elsewhere. Come and see me before the
Dasserah is over." It was the Yuvaraja, brother of the Maharaja and father of the present ruler of that state. How gloriously generous he was. Like everything else about this
handsome and kindly person, everything he said, all he gave,
whatever he touched, was from the heart. Big, warm and
human. No wonder he was so beloved by the peoples of
Mysore State. He had dash, elegance and a romantic aura.

The Yuvaraja was my first royal patron. And how grateful
I was for his interest and encouragement. I noticed on that

and Rajput father

"Sono Baba"

Ram Gopal's Burmese mother

At Chopin's house, 1938

first occasion when I danced at Lalita Mahal, that always hovering around the Yuvaraja was a bevy of beautiful women: blondes, brunettes, redheads, Austrian, English, French and Scandinavian. The Royal One chose his entourage like some racehorse owner would pick horses. The best, and most beautiful, besides the most elegant. And why not? Were they not happy to be favoured by so gracious and handsome a monarch as this Royal One?

I hid all of this excitement and adventure from my father. He would, I was certain, be furious. But later I told Mother secretly and quietly when the whole household had gone to sleep. She was amused and delighted. Her long slanting eyes sparkled with joy that her son had evoked so much enthusiasm. She never dampened my spirit, or my desire to dance. But Father! I was up against a stone wall. His son take to dancing? That ignoble and vile art that had so fallen from its original pedestal and purity, which only temple prostitutes danced, and offered other services with their body not strictly confined to the art of Hindu Natya. Unthinkable! "Why do you run around half-naked in those draughty rooms? Don't you know you'll get cold? All this monkeying and dancing? Why don't you go and play tennis or study or go for a walk?" He could never understand me as Mother did. It was no use, I gave up trying to argue or talk him into my way of seeing things. Mine was a world of dreams made manifest when my body moved in rhythm to the dance, and Father's world was far, far removed.

Months later I was sent for by my friend, Devarajurs. The Yuvaraja had requested that I dance again at a garden party in Bangalore. Would I do it? Of course I would. Father would never find out. It was exclusive. Besides, his world of Sanskrit pundits and literature was far removed from that of the court circle of the Royal One. I agreed to dance. The time was between five and sundown. Flares were lit in this

beautiful garden and banked by flowers on either side. To
the music of drums and flute I was again dancing as Siva when
from somewhere from out of that golden dusk, like the crack
of a whip, came the voice of my father. And he shouted,
make no mistake of that! How he got there, what the Royal
One thought about the enraged parent, I was only vaguely
told. It seems that some Brahmin in the staff of the royal
household had told some Brahmin on the staff of Father's
office that a singularly exact double of his son was dancing.
This particular Brahmin on the staff of my father had told my
father, so they had gone along to have a look. I never found
out how they got in. But at any Indian function 'by invitation only', then as now, be it a wedding, a Durbar, a funeral
or just a house party, anybody who really wanted to get in
was never turned away from the gates of the party giver. But
when I had heard that voice boom across the heads of the
Royal Ones and the respectable seated and silent audience, I
quickly parachuted to earth, leaving all those stars and moons
hanging in the sky of my dance. More quickly than any jet-
crashing pilot, head-dress and all leapt with me in the most
agile swiftness over innumerable beds of flowers, hedges and
fountains! I took all in my stride. I took a circuitous route
and instead of choosing the guarded entry of the gateway, I
decided to take the nearest tree to the lowest wall. Quick as
Hanuman, the monkey God, by some miracle, still perching
my head-dress on my head, I was up and over that last hurdle
. . . only to be confronted by a two-mile journey in the
darkening night to my home. I do not think Roger Bannister,
at that age and in those circumstances, precariously balancing
a head-dress on his head, could have made it with greater
speed. Poor Siva, in full flight! Traffic stopped, cyclists
turned, and pedestrians froze on the wide avenues of the road
Siva had decided to take for his flight. Undaunted, but
dropping with exhaustion and short of breath I arrived home

again over a wall. Straight to the fountain in the garden, a great gulp of water and like some trained tiger I sped up to my cage, my room on the first floor of the house.

The sequel is not without humour. Father stormed back roaring like some Rajput lion whose cub had disgraced him. I saw the headlights of a car swerve up the drive of our house. I heard Mother's eager questions. The secretary of the Royal One had been sent post-haste to appease the wrathful father of Siva, and with the personal assurances that it was only by 'royal request' that the boy had danced, did Father's temper abate. I think he was secretly amused. He must have been impressed by what he saw. But something of the Rajput in his blood must have revolted at seeing his son dancing nearly naked in front of the citizens of his home town, thus bringing, as he thought, disgrace upon his name and family. Yet with it all he was, I am sure, amazed that the Royal One had taken a personal interest in asking his son to perform. Perhaps, after all there was something in it all. . . . Perhaps . . . but nonsense, his son must be an Advocate . . . never, never the degrading profession of dancer. . . .

But somehow I was as determined to dance as Father was determined that I should not. After all, his fiery blood ran in my veins, and add to that the Mongolian streak from Mother's side. Yes, I would . . . and if he cast me on the streets, well what was so wrong . . . I would dance in the streets, anywhere . . . but I must, I would dance and nothing would stop me. "Mother, why does Father want me to do something I do not love or want to do? I would work all day and night at practising and dancing and I don't care if I never get paid, but why, oh why can't I dance and why must he be against me?" Time and again this was the theme song between son and mother, and as often mother would come back with the quick rejoinder: "But of course you must dance. You will admit it is different from studying law which

Father wants you to do. And you know, son, that the reports coming in from your school are absolutely shocking. Only in English, drawing and history are your results favourable. In everything else the teachers complain that you stare into space and wait patiently for that evening bell to ring. That you take no interest at all in your classes and that always your mind is far, far away. So be patient. Certainly dance. But let time console your father and leave the rest to me. I'll see what I can do with him."

Leave the rest to her? How often I had heard that from her when any of the large family wanted something out of Father. Mother always exercised her potent charm over Father.

Of course I danced again . . . privately. For garden fêtes and parties, for palace parties by moonlight and torchlight, in drawing-rooms and in half-ruined temples, dimly lit by oil lights to the heavy odour of incense and jasmine. And come what may, this is what I wanted to do and would continue to do. And I did. I think Father knew. But he pretended not to notice.

Then one Saturday afternoon as I was lazily resting under the spreading shade of a low hanging jasmine-scented arbour, the postman came towards me. He had a blue letter in his hands. It was for me. I turned it over, wondering who would want to write to me. It bore the royal crests of Mysore. It could be from no other than my Royal Prince himself. I guessed it was going to be another invitation to dance again for some big Dasserah Festival, or big festival event. I opened its pages. It was a letter from the Yuveraja himself asking me to come and see him at an appointed time and date.

"I have been thinking over for some time the possibility of taking a troupe of representative musicians and dancers to Rome and England and possibly Paris. Europe has never seen the dances from our state. I plan to take some hand-picked musicians and other folk dancers and I would like you to lead the dancers. Would you like to come? It will, you understand, take some time . . . plans have to be made."

"Oh, yes please. I would love to come. Of course I'll dance, it will be an honour. Are we leaving soon?" I asked enquiringly.

"Oh no, plans may take six months, possibly longer, I've so much official red tape to wade through for sanctioning finance and other matters. But don't worry. . . . It will be soon enough; time passes. . . . Glad you're eager and ready . . . I knew I could count on you."

My mind filled with excitement. Europe? London, Paris, and then to dance in Rome possibly for His Holiness, the Pope? Suddenly I felt that time was short. Besides, while these plans were being made by His Highness, I would have to get costumes. A bold thought seized me, and taking my courage into both hands, I openly asked: "Your Highness . . . while there is the planning and this wait . . . over the period of time . . . in the meantime . . . I wonder? Oh, but I . . ." the words faltered and froze. I could not make up my mind to ask what I wanted; what occupied and worried me.

"Yes, go on . . . what is it . . . you know you can talk to me and I can advise and try and help you."

I thought—I may as well come straight to the point. "Your Highness, you see . . . it is like this . . . Well, I don't know how to begin. . . . Well er . . . I want to work till I drop . . . you know how I have tried, you have been so kind . . . but, you see, I have no costumes. Not really. I cannot ask Father; he has given nearly all of his considerable fortune to my elder brother. There is nothing left for me. My mother has no money. . . . And—well I need money for buying head-dresses, costumes, instruments . . . and I would be so grateful if you could help me to get them. Oh, don't worry, I'll repay you." I had finished with a sigh of relief. Thank God that was over.

"But of course, my boy, I'll do what I can for you. No, don't bother to repay me. Your dancing is sufficient repayment. But never stop learning, go on and on, and promise you'll revive what has nearly been lost in Mysore State, in fact most of South India. I'll give you a few thousand rupees. Buy yourself all you need." And that was my first 'angel'. Given with a blessing from the heart. My face must have conveyed to him how earnest I was. My spirit soared with joy. What glorious costumes I would create and make and buy! With winged excitement I found myself gaily walking down the long, long drive. It was a pleasure, anyway, for the grounds of his palace were so beautiful. I had walked up the long driveway. I felt a bit shabby in my clothes, which I had pressed and cleaned to the best of their possibilities. But my cycle on which I had come to visit this King? I could never, never let him see that. I could not cycle up to the stairs of a castle and since I did not have a car or the money to hire one, I would leave it outside the palace gates and walk instead. Far more dignified. Much more simple. And that is the story of how the great Yuvaraja became the first patron I had ever known. I believe his good wishes and blessings carried me a long way.

Two thousand rupees! What a fortune that amount was to me then, in those years of the early 'thirties. What miracles I planned to achieve with them. Of course the first thing I did was to run straight back to Mother and tell her the good news. Within my bosom, held safely in a bulging envelope, were those green notes, like freshly-mown grass, I thought, only they would do for my dancing what grass would never, could never do. They would buy me the much needed equipment without which I could really do nothing.

I searched the lanes, streets and narrow alleys of the

market in Bangalore and found all the jewellery I needed, the silks, the various materials necessary to make head-dresses. I did not like what I saw some of the folk and traditional dancers wearing. They looked like something imposed upon them by Victorian missionaries. After all, the English missionaries discouraged any form of Indian dancing as 'devilish'. Where could I look for my patterns and jewellery designs? The big library in the park, accessible to all students. And there I went day after day, week after week. I got hold of a big book, with actual photographic studies and details of hand mudras and jewels. And I noticed its author's name was Gangoly. I met him years later and told him how his book had guided me in the choice of my first costumes. "You couldn't have chosen better, Ram. After all, they've been made and fashioned by the greatest artists of their day, and anything you have duplicated and copied from those bronze images, sculptures and the frescoe paintings that abound in South India and other parts, too, must be the most accurate." How right my intuition was in guiding me to copy the costumes of the Gods Siva, Krishna the Blue God, and Vishnu the preserver, to mention just a few names. I drew designs and traced others, and then carefully took them to the craftsmen I discovered, patiently sitting hour after hour, in their shops in dirty little back streets. Together we worked out each detail of the costumes. I would dress exactly like those wonderful dancing gods. After all, the dance was dedicated to them. And Lord Nataraja, God of the Dance, or Siva, as he is also called, what could be more authentic than to copy his costume? It had been there almost since the dawn of Indian Art, thousands of years ago.

In addition I had the idea that going first hand to the temples of Belur, Somnathpur and Halebid in Mysore State, would also give me ideas for costumes. The more I saw of their traditional costumes, the less I liked them. My reason?

I saw nothing remotely approaching the refinement and beauty of the temple sculptures and bronzes. And that, to any discerning eye was easily noticeable. Besides, then as now I wanted to move like the birds and tree-tops and fish and snakes and animals I loved. Who could watch their breath-taking grace if they were encumbered with clothes! And those gods on those temple walls frozen for all time in bronze, marble, ivory and wood, would be equally ill at ease if clothed. So let me be as naked as the bronze images allowed! Nobody, no Hindu, at any rate, could criticise such costumes, for after all it was those self-same and semi-naked divinities to whom they made oblations of milk, rice and flowers and prayers. And that in the beginning, was how I came to fashion my costumes.

I danced everywhere and anywhere for anyone who invited me. My means of locomotion was my cycle. Tied securely behind were my costumes on a carrier. And my beloved friend Krishna Rao, a superb dancer himself today, and my boyhood friend, would cycle side by side with me. He was the drummer. And what glorious times we had together. I would get a little money at these various recitals, also cakes and tea. But it was not that that made me happy. It was the fact that I could dance for people. The look on the faces of so many caste Indians seeing a boy assume divinity, and dancing for them on some green lawn in a garden was something I could never forget. Amusement, horror, disgust, finally interest . . . and usually at the end of the performance complete approval. It was new to them. Most Indians in the Mysore State referred to what they had seen of their native folk dances as 'Jungle dances by jungle people!!' "But your dance. Somehow it's different. Something quite new. More like the Gods themselves. And well . . . we just love watching you dance. . . ." Encouraging words! And I danced again and again tirelessly.

I combed by cycle, foot, bus and third-class train, in those days, every village, every corner of Mysore, Malabar and Tanjore district. The money I got from the Royal Prince was serving me in good stead. I determined to make good use of it. Each of the villages I visited had a wealth of dance. Temple dancing, folk dancing, street dancing. A former principal and teacher, a Mr. Pie, a professor from Cochin attached to one of the leading Ernakulum Universities, told me of the wonder and dynamism of Kathakali dancing. My first initiation into this unusual dance style was at the local town hall, where a troupe were performing. Mr. Pie took me to see it. The crude singing of the musicians jarred on my nerves, and the costumes and repetitive quality of the dancing became monotonous. But where in all of my life had drumming ever created the thunderous effect that the Chendai and Madallam did with those powerful clashing, giant-sized cymbals? And some of the whirling movements of the dancers, magnified by the particular Vasco da Gama skirts with the wild shrieks and shouts of the dancers, and the incredible language of the hands, made an unforgettable picture on my mind. I determined to learn all I could.

A third-class ticket, scant information, notebooks and pencil in hand, with a pathetic roll of bedding and a pillow, and off I went to the Kerala Kalamandalam School of the eminent, kind, laughing, humorous and very lovable poet genius of Malabar, Vallathol. How childlike he was! How readily he smiled, always for everyone, whether talking to some untouchable seeking advice or taking orders, or whether to one of the high-caste Brahmins visiting him. Always and ever kind, laughing and charming. He made a lasting impression on me. The way he watched those performances, like a child lost in the world of a fairy-story, his eyes riveted on the dancers, whether at rehearsals or during an all-night performance. Here was what I wanted. Vallathol was a Guru to be respected, loved, and from whom to learn. He was a storehouse of information. His poems, little snatches of which his sons translated for me, were full of wit and humour and truth. Then there was at this Kerala Kalamandalam School, Mukunda Raja. He was more serious, less easily impressed and seemingly more critical than Vallathol, but very erudite, nevertheless, in the great traditions and literature of Malabar. He was the right-hand man of Vallathol in reviving Kathakali. This whole school was dedicated to its reincarnation.

The 'school' I must hastily add was a pale blue-coated 'choonam' paint-washed building of some dozen or more rooms that housed kitchen, costumes, offices and some living-rooms, all very ascetic and simple. Outside, at some distance from the school, on the right-hand side was a thatched shed about half the size of a shrunken tennis court. The floor was watered daily and flattened down and washed over with cow dung. And clad in white loin cloths, pupils and Guru, or Maestro, would go through massage, eye exercises and the like, about which I will write later, and also full-length dance dramas, either in part or whole, before the critical eye of Vallathol. Again and again day after day, month after month. It took seven to eight years to get a good outline! No student ever laughed or smoked or joked. There was deep reverence in their whole attitude to learning this sacred art. And how they worked!

It was here that I first met the greatest living Kathakali actor-dancer, Kunju Kurup, and Hari Das, his son. I also saw the late Ravunni Menon, noted for teaching his men to dance like men. In fact his style was considered so virile and masculine that few of his pupils could keep pace with his exacting demands. There was the other teacher, Ambu Pannikar and a host of other lesser-known but accomplished dancers. Gopinath and Thankamani, who later became palace dancers in Travancore. Kalyaniamma, one of the few living women then to dance Mohini Attam, a sort of mixture between 'Deva Dasi Attam' of Tanjore and Kathakali. Most of her love songs (Padams) were taught her by my great teacher, Guru Kunju Kurup. He was and is unrivalled, not even remotely approached for the refinement, suggestion, humour and beauty of his 'abhinaya'. What a great actor!

There was every sort of folk dance that one saw from the various regions of Malabar itself and performed on various occasions. And this school, so simple, so dedicated was set amid thickly wooded casurina, mango, coconut and rice-studded groves and fields. And how it rained! One moment the sky was blue. The next instant there would be black clouds. Peals of thunder and lightning, and branches ripped from their trees, uprooted coconut trees, and roofs ripped off their humble dwellings; that was what the sudden rains did during Monsoon time. And snakes! They crawled around everywhere, of every shape and size. I remember how scared I got the first time I had a lesson, when gazing at the thatched roofing of the dance studio, I beheld a pair of murky, yellow topaz-coloured eyes looking rather sleepily.

"A snake!" I yelled, leaping lightly out of the shed.

Laughing my teacher said: "Oh that, it's Ananta, the rat-catcher. Don't worry, he won't bite. In fact, we feed him!" I grew used to and friendly with Ananta, but only after a long, a very long time!

When training under my gurus in their own towns I went to bed with the chirping of the birds as they settled themselves in the branches of the surrounding banyan and cashew nut trees between seven and eight o'clock at the latest, in the evenings. Hardly had my head touched the woven mat I slept on than I would fall asleep. And always in my sleep I was some God destroying all the dark devils that kept arising out of the shadows, or Rama, hero prince of the epic Rama-yana, wandering in forests accompanied by the beautiful Sita. Inevitably at two o'clock in the morning in the pitch black of our Indian night, I would feel the light touch of Kunju Kurup: "Son, get up, you've only half an hour to arise. Bathe your-self with some water and come and have some coffee or milk. We must work hard today." "We must work hard today." How many days, how many weeks, months, years, went into those words "We must work hard today, you've so much to learn".

Shaking myself out of sleep and fatigue, I would drag myself fumbling to the well, haul up buckets of cold water and often give myself a good splash with a bucketful of water to shock me into full wakefulness, and then rub myself down quickly with a towel. The nights at that hour in South India are chilly. Then, wearing my dhoti, a piece of white cotton around my waist and legs, I would go to the place of instruction.

In the simple thatched cottage of this great teacher, lessons began with eye practice. And often, I could not help feeling, had a third party seen what went on between my great Guru and myself 'making faces' by the light of kerosene lamps, they would have thought us quite mad. Kunju Kurup, with his right hand raised and forefinger extended, would move his arm with a circular motion first to the right, then left, then cross-ways, forming the figure eight and such-like patterns; all this sitting about three feet away from me. Without moving my head I had to follow with my eyes alone every single pattern that he traced with his forefinger in the air. How my eyes watered! But no matter, I could not stop to wipe away the tears that inevitably came during such practices. The more my eyes wept, the more certain Kunju Kurup was that I was performing these rigid exercises correctly. After about an hour and a half, with perhaps a quick interval or two in between, and after streams of tears had flowed from my eyes, Kunju Kurup would say: "The ghee I've used today must be good and much fresher than yesterday's, for your eyes are redder and you've been able to go on much longer today." By his side was a green banana leaf and by the end of the hour and a half of eye exercises the leaf would be empty of its spoonful of pure ghee. Most of the eye exercises had three tempos: slow, faster and very fast. But how refreshed and strong I felt at the end of these practices! And how my eyes gleamed, like two lights burning from within and filled with fire. I used to be so fascinated by them that when I caught a glimpse of them in a mirror they seemed truly to belong to those Gods my great teacher talked about always. It was with a start that I realised they belonged in my own face!

Towel wrapped round his head as was his custom, Kunju Kurup would now move closer to me and I could see by lamplight every single expression of his eyes, shining too, and feel his breathing. Taking what remained of the ghee, he would then massage my entire face and neck with his own hands, using all the muscles that give mobility to the face in the expression of the Kathakali dances: above the eyebrows, beneath the eyes, the cheeks, over and above and below both the lips and the sides of the neck. Then a specialised assistant of Kunju Kurup, a masseur trained in the science of the Ayur Vedic medicinal methods, would come in. After covering me liberally with gingelly oil, a sort of mustard oil strengthened with herbs and having a strange odour of its own, peculiar to Malabar, he made me lie face downwards. The masseur would then, with his right foot massage my spine from the base up and then round in semi-circular movements on both my right and left sides. This would be repeated right down to the extremities of my arms and legs. Then I would be made to turn over and, excluding the face the same movements would massage every single muscle of my body, the masseur supporting himself either on a bamboo stick to maintain his balance, or often holding on to some part of the low hanging thatched roof and maintaining an even balance as both feet worked on my body. This finished, and feeling extraordinarily light and toned up, I would be asked to rise and go through a lot of postures and rhythms that made for flexibility and a controlled co-ordination.

With the first light of early morning breaking in through the small windows, Kunju Kurup would order some fresh milk to be boiled. While this was done I would take another quick bath and be ready in a few minutes to join him for this early morning breakfast. Then he would tenderly ask me: "Did you sleep well last night?" Looking at him with surprised confusion, I would catch his eyes laughing, but his face was absolutely immobile. It was only by the corners of his mouth where I looked to see what mood he was really in, being the superb actor that he was, that I would know he was having a mild joke! There would be a one-hour break till about eight-thirty and then back again to the earthen floor, which is supposed to take the heat out of one's body and to be strengthening to the legs for the strenuous practices that went on all the time.

"Today you will be Krishna and I shall be your poor childhood friend Sudama who comes to beg for alms." Or, "You shall be the beautiful maiden Damyanti and I shall be your handsome prince Nala, and I want you to convince by every look, gesture and expression that you are truly, deeply in love with me." Occasionally he would say: "We've had enough of love this past week; now you shall become the terrible Ravanna and we will do battle." And so it went on, right through the varied and rich pantheon of Hindu Gods and demons. I was made to think, act, feel and become each of them and to believe that I 'was' some Divinity or Devil.

And I did. Most of the characters we enacted came out of those classics that every Hindu is versed in, the Ramayana and Mahabharata. When it got too hot at a little past midday we would retire for yet another bath. By way of a change I would plunge into the cool waters of a running stream or rivulet. Then a light lunch eaten off banana leaves and a rest for an hour. Then back again, inevitably, to more practice until early evening.

After dinner in the evenings we would sit cross-legged on the floor or on wooden stools and Kunju Kurup would teach me the hand gestures and facial expression only. These were the 'Mudra' sessions. Mudras are the elaborate gesture language of the hands by which the dancer tells a story. In the four main schools of Hindu dancing there are some five thousand single and combined double-hand Mudras, or gestures that have to be learnt precisely to produce that 'flow' that is such a characteristic of this form of dance.

Kunju Kurup kept repeating to me: "You must become, you must concentrate and feel so intensely all I tell you when we are working that you are not conscious of the self. The self is forgotten, unimportant, small, of this world. But that 'other self', the God you are portraying, must come to life by sheer will-power and concentration, and this is possible only if you are completely lost in the rhythm of the moment."

In my dance of Siva's Sandhya-nritta-murti, the dance that Siva performs at the setting of the sun, 'He, Lord of the evening dance', I could not help feeling in this purely personal dance creation of mine, in which I used the Kathakali technique, that I was on Mount Kailasa, those peaks first scaled by Tensing and Hillary. In this dance I had to convey the gentle rhythmic movements of the oceans, the winds and the twinkling stars of the evening and show the benign aspects of Nature at her best. With only the black curtains behind me I so immersed myself in Siva, the Divine Yogi, that I really

felt I was sitting in complete isolation on a solitary peak of
Mount Kailas. I was detached, free from all worldliness, lost
in a deep meditation, arising slowly to set the world to sleep
and to take and absorb into myself all the suffering, tragedy
and worry of the world. How could I convince an audience
that I was a God unless I had bewitched and enchanted myself? As Arnold Haskell, the critic, says: "You convince me
only because you yourself are filled with conviction." And to
achieve that, what a lot of endless work and study, suffering
and jealousy, it had cost me in my young life! And what a
little I had really known, and how despondent it would make
me, then as now, when I think of the little I was fortunate
enough to learn from my masters, as compared to their vast
oceans of knowledge.

For dancing is truly a visual 'rhythm of magic'. As in
Yoga, the dancer approaches, becomes 'one with' the Divine.
I have often felt myself enter another world. The magical
sounds from the clash of the cymbals, the plaintive notes of
the Veena and the throbbing golden beats of the Mridangam
accompanying the songs of the Gods which the musicians
sing, have all opened the ever present 'invisible dimension of
another world'.

I remember the first time I danced on the black cylindrical
marble floor of Belur, that ancient Hoysala monument built
by a king and queen for both of them to pray, meditate and
dance on during various temple rituals. What a trance I fell
into! I was conscious of the music, and of the silent faces of
the Indian spectators for a few brief moments, and then
gradually they seemed to dissolve, and in their place I saw
only mists and I was back at the very beginning of creation
when man's body sang in an ecstatic trance through the mute
language of the dance.

Whenever I could I watched dancers and dances in their
own setting. I saw the Ramanattam, the 'Ottam Thullal' solo

Bronze of the God Siva in his Dance of the Setting Sun

Bronze image of Shiva in the Great Temple at Tanjore

Ram Gopal as Siva in the Temple of Belur

village dance, half clowning, half satirical and the solo male dance, 'Seethan Gal Thullal' in which the dancer reminded me of a frilled lizard with his freshly cut and ornamented arm, head and wrist—the 'jewels' were made, I was told, from the tender bark of the banana trunk and also from the coconut shoots. In the temples itself I saw the 'Chakyar Kuttu' temple dance drama, recitations, chantings and mudras with elaborate facial expressions.

Male dancing is predominant in Malabar. It was and is still men who were and shall ever be the 'Gurus' or teachers. This I found out later on was true in every aspect of Hindu traditional art, be it music, dancing, literature or Yoga. Now and again a freak would appear, and learning from these male teachers in Malabar, would give a good imitation of how masculine a woman could attempt to be. But it was rare, though not unknown. I am talking here about women taking part in the traditional Kathakali dance dramas, make-up, costume and all. From first-hand knowledge, I know that any female studying, say, under Ravunni Menon or Ambu Pannikar, two of the teachers at the school of Vallathol, would be completely 'spoilt' for learning any other 'lasya' or lyrical type of Indian dancing. However, such a view is un-important, for it is the male dancer that is and ever will be supreme in the Kathakali dance.

In Tanjore I remember seeing in the village of Soolaman-galam the full-length dance dramas enacted with masks, head-dresses and make-up, a dance style called the Bhagavata Mela Nataka. In a way, this style is reminiscent of the Kathakali dramas. Only the music is more refined. The style of this Tanjore dance drama employs the very stylised and angular movements peculiar to this ancient dance tradition. And of course there was the 'Dasi Attam'—the female courtesan dance of Tanjore.

My guru, Meenakshisundaram Pillai, and Ponniah Pillai of

D

1880 West Main Street, in Tanjore, told me that the Solo dance known as 'Dasi Attam' was drawn up and created by their ancestors, a long line of dance instructors deriving much of their style and inspiration from the Bhagavata Nataka Mela Dance Drama performed by the Brahmin Priests. Today my good friend E. Krishna Iyer is again doing valuable research work in this ancient temple dance drama I had seen there so long ago. In Kumbakonam I saw Varalakshmi and Bhanu-mati, two sisters perform this 'Dasi Attam'. It was as delicate as the finest brush strokes of a Moghul Court Painter, as refined and languid as the Temple frescoes of Ajanta. They made an unforgettable impression on me.

I saw other forms of folk and temple dancing and ritual, too numerous to mention. Suffice it to say that after a period of studying first hand and seeing the great dance traditions of the south I was now, thanks to my Royal Prince's patronage, well equipped to give recitals of my own. Being born of a Rajput father I yearned to go to Jaipur, Ajmere, Bikanneer in the north and study my father's regional and Tribal court and folk dances one day. I had come back with notebooks full of the most complicated dance patterns, symbols, ciphers and scribbling all of which was only decipherable to me. It was my own method of notating all I had seen!

Travelling third class in those uncomfortable and badly ventilated compartments, going by foot through the most remote villages and through jungle pathways, by bullock cart and on horse-back, searching, seeing, studying and working, had all helped me to absorb the atmosphere of my beloved south into my personality.

Unlike other dancers before me, I was the first to be privileged to give all honour and due to whatever I was able to learn from the feet of those great dance masters who were the treasure-houses of knowledge and learning. And it was only later, much later, when I toured India in several nation-wide tours that I took along my guru, Kunju Kurup, with me, and talked, lectured and demonstrated with him in the Sanskrit universities of Allahabad, Benares, Lahore and other centres in the north of India. The amazed students and professors of those universities had the first-hand experience of seeing something that they never dreamed existed: a supreme dance style, mime, gesture, expression and technique that moved them all, everywhere, to wonder. This, aside from the public seasons I gave everywhere in nearly twelve nation-wide tours, from the tip of Ceylon to the far reaching theatres or halls of Peshawar and from Bombay to Calcutta.

I was back in Bangalore. "You look like a creature possessed," said my parents and sisters. "What happened? What is it that makes you look so happy?" I told them for long, long hours, sitting at dinner, at lunch and in that beautiful garden that Mother had created. Then I danced for them in a converted hot-house that I had lit with oil lights and converted into a sort of improvised dance studio. And they were seeing for the first time how serious was their youngest son.

"His Highness wants you to come and dance." Enigmatic, smiling, happy, it was my friend Devarajurs again. Nothing more, nothing less. Just that. Come and dance! Perhaps all this time he had been good enough to wonder about the little boy he had patronised and helped, who had gone off searching for the dance. It could be that he wanted to see if all that time I had been away had been put to good use, and if so, what I had made of it.

"When?" I replied. "Any time you wish, any evening after ten, that is," replied my friend.

"But I am in bed by nine," I replied.

"Then you'll have to make it later. His Highness wants to see you dance, and dance you must for him. And you will have to make the time suitable to him."

"All right," I said. "Let me know when."

"Let's make it Saturday." And that was how that Saturday, days later I danced for my Royal Prince and Patron.

"You've done wonders, Ram Gopal. I wish we didn't have to wait so long now for that European tour which I spoke about to you before. But all this red tape and official this that and the other. Sometimes I wish . . . sometimes I wish I were just an ordinary citizen to do as I please."

He looked both pleased at my dancing and impatient at the slow, inexorable machinery of officialdom that seemed, I sensed, to be holding things up.

"Your Highness, how long do you think we may go on this tour and possibly when?"

Impatiently, but kindly, looking at me, he answered: "I don't really know. Six months. Longer maybe. Years for all 'they' care . . ." He broke off. "Have a drink, Ram Gopal. Let us drink to your future." More of that 'bubbly stuff' was ordered. It was champagne. I loved it. I knew that this connoisseur of life, wine, women and song, would want and have nothing but the best, and believe me that pre-war champagne really made one see stars. It lifted me right out of myself. I felt floating.

Destiny and Fate had other plans for me. I had danced in November and December of 1936 at the large local theatre, called the Opera House, which showed Metro Films. Here one day I danced at a charity performance. I was so grateful and so encouraged. Mr. Cooper, the Parsi Manager, had become good friends with me. A few weeks later I was at the Cantonment station seeing off a friend of mine on her way to Madras. Her train had left and I was walking back towards the exit. There was a tap on my shoulder, it was Mr. Cooper, the Parsi who owned this so-called Opera House. "Come and meet the dancer, La Meri" . . . We walked across and were introduced. A well-built woman in her mid-thirties stood in front of me. Beautiful blue eyes and the figure of a tennis champion, an athlete. The most nasal drawl I had ever heard issued from her in a friendly greeting.

Daily after that, during her season at the Opera House in Bangalore I taught her all she ever knew of Kathakali, as she had never been to Malabar, did not intend to go there, and preferred to learn, anyway, from me directly. Finally it was decided that after hearing her enthusiastic talk of her forthcoming Far East tour, my parents agreed that I could join her.

"Of course, you understand that you will not be paid anything. Your father can give you an allowance and after we reach Japan, by which time you will learn all there is to know of stagecraft, you will be paid a salary." Those were the kindly words of encouragement I got from her Italian husband!

"He'll be begging for his return passage in a few months," said my father as I got ready to depart. But my mind was made up. I would join her. It would mean the hard way, the going would be tough, but I was determined not to flinch.

I have heard a lot of people talk about the discomforts of touring the English provinces. I have toured around them three times myself. But believe me, they spell luxury with all their discomfort and squalor when compared to touring and living in the kind of 'Dug-out Digs' I lived, travelled and worked under at this time. Perched high up on her loaded lorry full of costume trunks, to and from boats and stations, sweeping the stage, and helping to clean, put up and remove her black velvet tabs, these and lots of other jobs were mine during that period of apprenticeship. We visited all the big cities in India and then from Calcutta went on to Rangoon, Malaya, Java, the Phillipines, China and finally Japan. Everywhere I was studying the dances which this dancer attempted to learn.

"It's just a routine! I have a knack of picking up, notating and getting the proper costume," she would say. In my opinion she completely ignored the spiritual and mental attitude and consequently her interpretations were more mental than 'under the skin' studies, authentic as they were.

Everywhere I absorbed the atmosphere of all those great countries of the East. Always I visited every temple of antiquity, and every museum, and I studied and absorbed not only the dances, but also the spirit underlying them all. In her Hindu numbers, we danced to 'canned' music. We got rave notices, as also did my solos 'Siva', 'Indra' and 'Peacock', Kathakali-styled dances.

It was an exciting lesson to watch La Meri put on her make-up, or should I say change her face with the flick of an eyebrow pencil and lipstick to suit the numerous characters she attempted to portray. I thought how intelligently and swiftly she changed! She was a Hula dancer one moment, then Spanish the next, and as quickly changed to Russian ballet technique. Now she appeared as a Mexican doing the 'Jarabe Tapatio', dancing on the brim of her hat, then she was a Nijinski faun, a Marwari Nautch woman, a Burmese belle, a Javanese princess, the Spirit of a lake, a mechanical straw doll, mechanical lifeless, still. I am only mentioning a few of her numbers. There were dozens more of these three and four minute 'numbers' that filled her seemingly inexhaustible repertoire of dances. I began to think as time went on, as we moved from country to country, that there was something very entertaining and clever about what she did, and she did it with every ounce of conviction and sincerity of which she was capable. But I felt that if it took Pavlova a lifetime to perfect one technique alone, as it did with Nijinsky and Karsavina, and my great masters in India, how could any dancer attempt to present an 'Evening of the World's Dances?'

Nevertheless, the first-hand experiences I had of watching, learning, working and suffering the most abominable discomforts compared to home all prepared me for the future. So many Indian dancers want the 'soft way' and imagine that fame, success and money pour in at the box office by the very fact that they have to just appear and dance and that they will get the 'red carpet' treatment from press and public alike! Many Indian dancers suffer under this misapprehension and the few who have tried have had disastrous results, unless like Uday Shankar they started learning from the beginnning with humility and hard work.

The tension and uneasiness I had unerringly felt, broke in Japan. We had given three public recitals at the Hibiya Hall in Tokyo. Naturally I had danced my best. This was the very first time in the history of the Japanese Theatre that a Hindu, dancing his age-old legends, had appeared there, and I would become Siva himself.

"You must always try and give everything to the public, it's all that counts, honey." In this way La Meri told me in that Texas drawl that I had to 'do my very best!' Well I did. And I rode straight into a black and turbulent storm.

It all happened because a critic, voicing his opinion in the leading Tokyo paper had written the following:

"The closing section of the recital was given to six racial dances, of which the three Hindu numbers and the American Indian Hoop Dance starring. In this part of the programme, the audience in no uncertain applause demonstrated their unreserved admiration for Ram Gopal. . . . Without question he is the drawing card for these dance recitals. Tokyo has never been privileged before to witness such skill and genius. He is the Soul of Genius, a born dancer, and has the physical form of the perfect dancer: He is beautiful to behold in every movement. One regretted much that he was limited to one meagre solo dance and one performance with La Meri. The audience vigorously demanded an encore from the Hindu, but it was not granted.

"La Meri is a perfect dance technician, but her movements and interpretations failed to arouse enthusiasm in this reviewer, though she is delightful and enjoyable. Her physical proportions are not adaptable to beauty in the form of dancing. Her conceptions are intellectual to a high degree but lack somewhat in soul."

The name of the critic? An Englishman, I. J. Fisher, whom I had never before heard of or met. Friends said that he had written rave notices about Argentina, the Spanish dancer, and about Pavlova on one of her last visits to Japan, but this was one of the finest.

Here is another review from the *Musical Courier*, dated November 1st, 1937, titled: 'American Dancer Scores'.

"An American dancer, La Meri, with her Hindu protégé Ram Gopal, gave three recitals at Hibiya Hall. La Meri pleased the few people that came. The Hindu is a genius in native dances of his country. Already, La Meri has left for America and for some reason Ram Gopal is left stranded here and is being cared for by the local Hindus."

All this 'skill and genius' left me one morning standing on a street corner. . . . All I had was two boxes of costumes and the suit I was wearing. I was waiting for friends who would come and take me in their car to the house of an old lady. The day before my Indian friends gave me some money . . . told me not to worry . . . whatever happened they would not let me down. I could count on their friendship.

How those parting words rang in my ears: "You can dance your way back to India doing cabaret in some hotels, maybe you'll get engagements. . . ." With these words, the troupe had packed and left for America. And I had dreamed of dancing in America. Instead I was standing on that street corner, waiting for my friends. What if they did not arrive . . . where would I go, what would I do . . . I grew panicky. The warnings of my parents rang in my ears. Should I wire back to Mother and Father and tell them that their premonitions and warnings were right? Tell them that I had failed, though why, I could not understand, could not grasp. Search though I did, I felt innocent. I had worked hard, practised, taught this dancer everything of her Kathakali dances she knew, partnered and arranged all the choregraphy of the two numbers we danced in, and had helped backstage in every single job given me. I had done my best to please my elder employers, and yet the more I did, and the better I danced, as I was urged to in rehearsals, the more unfriendly they became. And I was put into this plight apparently because of that review in the papers. How I regretted that review! And I kept thinking: 'God moves in a mysterious way His works to perform. . . .' Well, that Great Father would have to perform a very, very big miracle to save me.

Had I only known that this drastic twist of fate, seeming so overwhelming at that time, was in fact to change the whole course of my career, my life, and my art! My star was in the ascendant. I was in the agony of rebirth, for as the tears filled my eyes with homesickness and I was in the depths of despair and loneliness, the stars above were dancing. I had to summon up all the teachings of the Gita, and Eight Fold Path of Buddhism, with my recollections of the Sage of Arunachala and all his teachings of the insignificance of the Self. Over and over again I kept searching out, repeating and chanting to myself the passages of these holy scriptural sayings, hoping to get comfort from them. But try as I did, the words were empty, cold, meaningless and hard . . . even cruel. The fact remained that I was starving, penniless, hungry and cold.

The long, tiring Far Eastern tour and the dangling hopes I had been led to believe would crown my months of hard work, teaching and loyalty, all lay shattered. So this was my reward! I walked as fast as I could to the nearest park, and there sitting down alone on a bench, I rested to review my plight . . . tears came to my eyes, I tried to fight them. It was useless. My will-power could not stand it any longer. I broke down and cried . . . all those pent-up feelings of humiliation, frustration, fear and failure gripped me. I felt hot all over. Perhaps the shock has caused this, I thought. It was instead a good blazing fever that was to lay my body down for a good long rest in bed. That night, a kindly lady, Mrs. Casey, put me up in her home. The next day I became worse. Mrs. Casey had met a Polish journalist, Alexander Janta, poet and nobleman of an ancient Polish family. He heard what had happened. Realising she could not do much, as she was poor herself, he invited me to take one of the rooms in his little Japanese house. There, for several weeks I lay ill. But with the kindly and restful attention of my friend, I grew stronger. To me that period was a nightmare . . . and to this day the recollection of those times fills me with fear and disgust. Shortly after my recovery I met an English gentleman, John Gadsby, legal adviser to the British Embassy in Tokyo, who was living there with his family in a house crammed full of the most wonderful Chinese Jades and Japanese works of art. Unhesitatingly he offered me all the help necessary. This was to be utilised for touring Japan, America and Europe if I so desired. Later I was told by John Gadsby that I could go to India and gather a troupe there for touring the West. Perhaps God, the Father in Heaven, had made the miracle come to pass. This was it, for even when things seemed darkest I met two of the most wonderful friends a young boy could have.

CHAPTER THREE

Indian Dancing and its Adaptation for the Theatre

SINCE the dawn of Indian civilisation, thousands of years ago, dancing has been a part of the life of Hindus in the north and south of that vast subcontinent. To anybody seeking a clue to the Hindu dance, it is well worth while to study in minute detail the ancient South Indian Pallava and Chola bronzes depicting Siva, God of the dance, poised in his tremendous dance of Creation, Preservation and Destruction. The fluid lines, so lithe and yet so powerful of the entire body, the static expression of the face, and the symbolic hands holding the sacred fires and promising salvation, all express dancing within the Torana (arch of fire); and surely this is the most majestic conception of the rhythmic movement of the universe. There is on view at the Indian section of the Victoria and Albert Museum, one of the finest South Indian bronzes of a dancing Siva made by Indian craftsmen centuries ago. All Indian dancing is woven around the Lives of the Great God Siva, the Divine Dancer whose dance depicts the cosmic universe in Action; Krishna, the Blue God, or Divine cowherd of North India; and Vishnu, the Preserver of this Earth.

An apt description of Siva's dancing, and of the God himself, reads thus: "The movement of whose body is the world, whose speech the sum of all language, whose jewels are the moon and the stars." There are a number of other gods and goddesses following in an endless train, performing various dances. The male deities perform the Tandava (masculine) style of dance, and the female the Lasya (feminine) aspects of this rare art. Parvati, Mohini, Sarasvati, Kali, Lakshmi, Urvashi are some of the notable goddesses, and Indra, Arjuna, Vishnu, and Ganesh, some of the gods.

The traditions of Hindu dancing go back into the remote past, and it is hard to tell how much of the divine origin attributed to the gods themselves in teaching the dance is myth, and how much fact. One can only look into the Sanskrit works in some of the great university libraries of Tanjore and Malabar, Benares and Baroda. As the genuine and classic dance stands today in South India one can trace its origin back to the Natya Shastra, the monumental and ancient text dealing with dancing music, rhetoric, grammar and allied subjects. It is clearly pointed out in this great work how the dancing came to be taught on this earth. Indra, after many meditations and prayers, was allowed the vision of Brahma, whereupon he asked Brahma to teach him for the benefit of Mortal man a new Veda (science). Brahma created the Natya Veda, or science of dancing, and entrusted Bharata Muni, a great sage, with acquainting mortals with it. Hence it has been known up to the present day as Bharata's Natya Shastra, meaning the science of dancing as laid down by the sage Bharata. The three forms of dancing expounded in this great work are *Natya*, which is drama, plot and story; *Nrtta*, pure dance or the release of energy through a series of rhythmic dance steps, and *Nrtya* which possesses flavour, suggestion and mood. And all the above styles of dancing have their *Tandava* (masculine) aspects, and in their more delicate forms the *Lasya* (feminine) aspects.

There are four main schools of Indian dancing today. The Kathakali dance dramas of Malabar performed by an entire troupe of dancers and musicians are all male. The Kathak dancing of Delhi and Jaipur which is mostly a solo dance; the Manipuri dance of Assam, lyrical and graceful in character; and the Bhagavata Mela Nataka Tanjore, all-male temple dance drama.

All Indian dances have a definite theme, unfolded with rhythmic sequence of music expression (*abhinaya*) and *mudras* (symbolic hand gestures of one or both hands). The *Rasa*, or Mood, is the basis of all Indian dance. Rasa means, literally, essence or flavour. Nine different moods cover the whole gamut of emotions employed by the face of the Indian dancer. They are as follows:

1. *Shringara*, the Erotic Sentiment
2. *Rudra*, the Furious Sentiment
3. *Veera*, the Heroic
4. *Vibhasa*, the Disgusting
5. *Hasya*, the Comic
6. *Karuna*, the Pathetic
7. *Adbhuta*, the Marvellous
8. *Bhayanaka*, the Terrible
9. *Shanti*, the Peaceful

All these nine sentiments bring into play the eyebrows, eyelids, nose, cheeks, lips and neck, of the qualified Indian dance artist, in exact rhythms and harmony with the symbolic gestures of the hands and the rhythmic beats of the feet.

The dance drama of Malabar, dynamic and potent with meaning, is known as Kathakali. It is a complex art, combining *abhinaya* (acting), dancing, and *gita* (music). It is a pantomime wherein the actors interpret their thoughts and

emotions through the highly sensitive medium of gestures
and extraordinary facial expressions, perfectly intelligible
even to the uninitiated. This style contains an elaborately
codified system of expression, silent, yet far more eloquent
than speech. There has long been a controversy amongst
scholars and critics of South Indian dancing as to which is the
older dance of Malabar—Kathakali, or the temple dance
known as Kodiattam. Both employ very much the same technique, gesture and expression. The chief differences are in
the musical accompaniments and themes. The Kathakali
orchestra is composed of three musicians, a vocalist who
sings the story enacted by the dancers, and two drummers
playing respectively the *Chenda*, and *Maddalam*, two cylin-
drically shaped drums that are capable of the most subtle
nuances as well as dynamic sounds.

A few hundred miles to the north of Malabar one sees an
entirely different type of people and the form of dancing
known as the Bhaga vata Mela Nataka, and the Dasi Attam.
Until very recently, the art of the Bhagavata Mela Nataka and
its solo courtesan derivative dance, the Dasi Attam, had been
performed by temple dancers. In the Bhagavata Mela Nataka
of Soolamangalam one sees the Tanjore equivalent of the all-
male Kathakali dance of Malabar. Only the music and gestures and costumes are less dynamic but more subtle and
hieratic, in gesture and expression. In its cruder Tanjore
solo dance, one sees the Dasi Attam, the dance of the temple
courtesan or prostitute dancing to ensnare the beholder with
sensual grace and charm with an emphasis on the *Shringara*
Rasa (Sentiment of the Erotic). Of the two Tanjore styles
the all-male Bhagavata Mela Nataka is by far the superior in
that it represents all the nine rasas, or sentiments, like the
Kathakali dance dramas, and another aspect is that this higher
form of Tanjore temple dancing allows only men to perform. Female characters are impersonated by men far more

effectively than by some modern female exponents of Kathakali, who give a crude performance 'impersonating' male
Kathakali characters.

Kathak is the dance art of North India. It is performed by
both sexes and once flourished in the courts of the Moghul
Emperors. The technique is vastly different to other types
and there is a strong Moghul influence in dress and ornament.
Let us watch a Kathak dancer in a performance. Still as a
statue, the dancer stands with feet crossed, the right arm
extended from the shoulder, the left held over the head. The
plaintive notes of a *Sarnagi* (stringed instrument) accompanied by the rhythmic beats of the tablas (drums) stirs the
dancer to mobility. As if touched by a breath of wind, in a
second the body sways and stirs gently, a ripple runs down
the arms, the eyes sparkle and come to life, the eyebrows
arch, the body gradually awakens to activity. As the arms
trace sinuous patterns, the ankle bells send forth jingling
sounds, first faint and then loud. Faster and faster move the
feet and in even rhythm with them the swift lightning turns
unfold the skirts of the costume as the dancer whirls and stops
and starts whirling again.

The Manipuri School of dancing in Assam is chiefly notable
for its softness and sweetness. It employs in its feminine
aspects great lyrical beauty, and fluidity of arms and body.
When well danced, one sees the dancer travel imperceptibly
from one movement to another without actually being aware
of the transition. The face is always mask-like, unlike the
three other schools of dancing. The *tandava* aspects of this
dance are performed with great power and require skill and
lightness of foot in execution. One notable feature of the
tandava form of this dancing, is the semi-seated posture in
which a man executes the most incredible spins, leaps and
jumps with comparative ease. But here again, as in the
other schools of Indian dancing, great skill and restraint is

required, and it takes as many as eight years to become an adept.

It is in the remote villages of Southern India, Tanjore and Malabar, the colourful villages of Rajputana, and the wooded villages of Manipur that the highest possibilities were developed and preserved for centuries down to this day. It is here that ancient dance lore handed down from father to son, both written and unwritten, has preserved in all its full- ness and profundity of histrionic expression, the strength and beauty of the art of Nataraja, God of the Dance, who requires that his disciples serve him in all simplicity, their souls pulsating with the Joy of God, Nature and Art. It is thus that all dance aspirants should approach this ancient art, dedicating themselves in all humility to Nataraja, 'Lord of the Dance'.

There are, in addition to these classical styles of dancing, a whole series of innumerable and colourful folk dances in every village and corner of India. Some of the earthy beauty of this dancing, performed with large groups of peasants, both men and women, is so breath-taking and exciting that in many cases they surpass the more refined temple dance in verve and rhythm and colour.

With the assured and perfected technique acquired from my great masters, after years of study I eventually felt con- fident and justified in taking Hindu dance into the theatre. I must say I was at first very startled to find that the public reaction to their native dances in Malabar, as also in Tanjore and Tanjore district itself, was one of indifference and bore- dom. Here as elsewhere in India, the Indian films with their power over the Indian masses had completely 'spoilt' their good tastes for something more sentimental, sugary and easier to understand.

"Mr. Ram Gopal, you are a lover of something that is dead," I was told by a professor at the Sanskrit University in

Cochin. "True, you are doing noble work in sacrificing your life in hard work and devotion. But then you are an artist and a dreamer. I am not, I am a practical man, and representative of the India of today, of now, and why should I want to know what those *mudras*, expressions and dances mean? I read my *Bhagavad Gita*, and in my mind I see and know enough of God and Truth. Those dancers, mechanical dolls, painted, decked and stuffed, whether in Kathakali or *Dasi Attam* are very limited in their appeal. In fact they are lifeless, dead and tiresome. You have revived the classic and creative side of these dances, and Shankar, who lacks your command of technique in the traditional sense, has given his creations of power and beauty. But tell me honestly, if you had not studied these dances, if you did not know what each gesture and expression mean, would you not feel like I do?"

Could the onlooker, completely devoid of academic knowledge of the dance, and worse, not interested in the 'Devil-like' masks, grimaces and crude Kathakali and erotic Tanjore temple dances ever understand? Here, certainly, was a point of view.

"Why," I asked the professor, "do you find the Hindu dance devoid of charm and beauty? And you tell me you speak for untold thousands all over India. Don't you see its subtlety, beauty and power?"

"Ram Gopalji, you know, because you've learnt," he answered. "I don't have any desire to learn, nor have I the time to try or want to know. I want to see something that does not bore me or embarrass me with the endless repetition of the Indian dancers' movements. And can you blame me, or the vast Indian public? You see we have changed too. Oh, I know you're going to tell me that the tradition must be kept pure and all that. Lots of fake dancers, and critics of the worst kind, have taken up the refrain from you and Shankar, but that's no good. The dance of the temples and

E

village is only a fragment of the Sanskrit drama and theatre as
it has come down to us. Besides, the temple theatre and the
ancient dance in India were created for another rhythm of
another age long since dead. Don't you think we should step
forward and create something that is understandable in terms
of today?"

"I don't entirely agree," I replied, "but I see your point of
view."

He was so right in many ways. I had seen my great guru
Kunju Kurup, perform his wonderful roles in Kathakali
dancing. I had seen those of the audience who understood
the Kathakali singing in Malayalam, sit up and take notice. I
had also seen the *pundits* of South Indian classical music and
dance at my side, and a large part of the Indian audience,
yawn, stretch, look over its shoulders to see what was going
on at the back, and in fact look everywhere but at the stage
where the miraculous dancing of Kunju Kurup was taking
place, and I wondered why the audience were getting restless
and bored. The answer was obvious: those who did not
understand the Malayalam language of Malabar were frankly
bored by the Kathakali dancers on the one hand, and others
were openly laughing at the 'faces' that they accused the actors
of making, not only at each other, but also at the audience!
And they were all Indians too. And with variations of reaction in the big cities of Bombay, Calcutta and Delhi, I
found that, generally speaking, the public reacted likewise to
the Tanjore temple dance drama, the Manipuri and the
Kathak dance. Only a handful of the audience appreciated
the great art before them. The rest either scurried fast from
the theatre, or, as in New Delhi during the 1944–5 All India
Dance Festival, started hooting the late Ravunni Menon off
the stage. Needless to say, they were North Indians from the
Punjab, and Sikhs, and would not tolerate this 'Devil
dancing' of the south which was called Kathakali. Uday

Shankar was not far wrong when he said that his success was due to a carefully planned, timed and executed modern programme, incorporating the old gestures and steps with new variations and his own personal style which is lyrical and fluid, added to a superb modern Indian orchestra.

During my student years with my great masters, then, I realised that I would have to prune the traditional dances of all repetitive movement, light the stage adequately, and costume my dances and ballets with the best available copies of the frescoes and sculptures and bronzes that my tailors could duplicate. I was never satisfied with the crudely-made jewels and ornaments that are used in the traditional dances of today in the four main schools. After a minute observation and detailed search of the bronzes, sculptures and paintings, in the temples scattered all over India, and the cave paintings of Ajanta and Sigiriya in Ceylon, I sought to capture the fine and brilliantly coloured robes, ornaments, and jewellery depicted in these most authentic references that were, beyond doubt, far superior to what most of the actor dancers wear in the four styles of the Indian Dance today.

That was how I designed and created my Setting Sun head-dress of the God Siva; also for the Cosmic dance of Creation, Preservation and Destruction, for which I duplicated the famous head-dress, since so widely copied by other dancers in India, in heavy gilded bronze and gold, down to the exact detail. Similarly for my Kathak dances of Rajputana and the north of India, I scrutinised the fine Moghul paintings in the museums of the cities of the north, and from them designed my Moghul Rajput Court dresses. In the Kathak dances of Lucknow and Delhi today one sees a vulgarised costume, more a mixture of the Turkish harem and Persian styles, than Hindu—a loose pantaloon affair, topped by an ungainly shirt.

The female dancers in my troupe were seldom allowed to wear the trussed-up, apron-fronted nine yards sari used in the

Tanjore courtesan dance, the 'Dasi Attam'. Instead I was the
first to design the spreading fan and blouse effect that has
since again been copied as the standard costume for women
dancers. . . .

In presenting Kathakali, Tanjore temple dances, Kathak
and Manipuri, on the modern stage in India, I learnt much
from watching the dance creations of Shankar, inasmuch as I
trimmed down the endless repetitions of gesture and song,
and tried to make the dancers do as much dancing as possible,
interspersing their *abhinya* acting, and thus achieving less
monotony. In the Tanjore dances, I always took good care in
India to choose those dances for the theatre-going public of
Bombay, Delhi and Calcutta, such as Invocation, a purely
rhythmic sequence, followed by a Svara-Jathi, a rhythmic
dance sequence, again with scintillating passages of fast
changing dance patterns. I also used the Natanam Adinar,
the Dance of Siva in the Tanjore style, again trimming its
monotonous repetition and using three pure passages of
rhythmic dance in that classic style.

In my programme for the Edinburgh Festival of 1956, I
gave a series of authentic folk dances from various provinces
of India, seen for the first time outside India, and only recently
in India itself, but I took good care to intersperse the programme with Kathakali extracts in traditional costume and
style and music by giving items like 'Dhusasana and Bhima',
an awesome dance spectacle in which Bhima slays and dis-
embowels Dhusasana. The other item on the repertoire for
the 1956 Edinburgh Festival and at the recent London season
was Sita Apaharan, or 'Abduction of Sita'. But in this case
Satyavati and Namboodri, both from Malabar, with a lifetime of study behind them, performed this with one difference. In Kathakali feminine roles are usually taken by boys
or men suitable for such parts. And in my innovation I had a
genuine Malabar girl, trained in Kathakali by great teachers,

perform the feminine role. There is, however, a deplorable tendency in India today for some very vigorous female dancers to perform male *tandava* (masculine) steps, in female garb, giving the impression of male impersonators of this highly masculine art. Such is the confusion today in the minds of a large section of the public both in India and abroad that this travesty of dancing has been taken for 'the real thing'!

In my programme, 'Dances of India', the Tanjore temple dances concentrated mostly on the rhythmic portions, with a few episodes of Sri Krishna and the Dances of Siva. There are several items of Kathak and Manipuri also adorning the collection of dances in this programme, and in addition to the traditional dances my own creations 'The Dance of the Setting Sun' and 'Garuda, the Golden Eagle' which the public always insists on. To balance the traditional programme of my Dances of India—a very difficult thing indeed—I had to construct the programme with enough variety and change to prevent the public from seeing too much instead of leaving them wanting more, a thing most Indian dancers and musicians find hard to do, for they always dance that much longer and play their instruments that much more monotonously to find that the public in India and abroad get impatient.

It is only when dancing in front of the few great *pundits* of the drama and dance in India, be it Tanjore or Malabar, that one can perform the full unedited work of a three or six-hour programme without breaks, and keep the select audience interested. The reason is simple. They understand either Tamil, Sanskrit or Malayalam. But the big public of India or the West does not understand these various dialects, and hence the monotony and boredom that engulfs the spectator. What is true of the Hindu dance, is true of the Spanish and traditional Russian ballet dance, and other forms, be they Chinese or Japanese, to the uninitiated theatre-going public of the West or the East today.

CHAPTER FOUR

First American Tour

MARTHA GRAHAM, that pioneer of American modern dancing, once said to me: "America is many nationalities, West and East, all merging, seeking, moving in rhythm, all of which I try and capture in the spirit of today. I use both forms and draw from both the western rhythm of the dance and certainly from the eastern, too. America is washed by the Atlantic on the one side; on the other, the warm waters of the Pacific caress us."

The warm waters of the Pacific caress us. . . . Well, it was *via* the Pacific that I had come to America. I had waved to Mount Fujiyama in Japan sadly. I had in my mind been ignorant and confused about the approach, and forgotten that it was the Pacific and not the Atlantic. I kept looking out for the Statue of Liberty, as we neared the coast of the New World.

"Say, is this the wardrobe of a man or woman?" a casual, burly, tough-looking Customs officer demanded. "What's this stuff?" drawing a Javanese *kris* or sword acquired there during my tour. "And this, and this . . . and this," and so he went right through my strange and exotic assortment of stage costumes. In the end, formalities over, my friend Janta and

I stepped into a car, after carefully trusting our luaggge to a travel agent, and sped off for Hollywood. The kindly wife of the American Ambassador in Tokyo, Mr. Grew, had given me precious letters of introduction to Cecil B. de Mille. And Rubinstein, the great pianist, said that he would influence the powerful Hurok to give me a season in New York.

In my pockets were those precious letters. One was to Cecil B. de Mille, and some other notables of the famous film capital. As the car sped towards the movie city, I could not help thinking of the great film stars. Would I meet any of them, I wondered! Aside from the film world, I would also meet Max Reinhardt, that genius of the European theatre and stage. I was fortunate, I was happy and people were kind.

How strange and wonderful the land and the smiling people of California were to me, and how sunny and blue the skies were, how wide the open spaces of the land. Nothing was cramped. Everything was big, bigger than I had seen till then. I had not yet seen how soaring those architects' dreams were and how man's ingenuity, cramped for space, could send buildings heavenwards in New York. It certainly was a land of plenty, and of friendliness.

One night in March 1938 I was seated at dinner with the supreme showman of Hollywood films, Cecil B de Mille. He took me around his house, filled with so many relics and antiques of rare beauty and value. I remember the various models he showed me of his then recent film *The Crusades*, and with what detail he explained each of the tireless researches he had made in order to satisfy his exacting sense of perfection. No pains were ever spared, money was no object, but everything had to be exact and perfect. He was handsome, with the distant, detached, cool look of a sage, a seer, a sort of *rishi* of the cinema world. But whatever he had to say on or about his religious outlook on life would be through his chosen medium, the films. And he was kindly. There was

very little of the great 'I Am' so typical of the chain-cigar
smoking, nauseating people of some film organisations.
Everything about him was outsize; and yet he was simple and
kind. I was reminded, now and again that he had the same
gentleness and simplicity as Gandhi.

"I have a deep respect for your country, her arts and the
great works such as the *Gita* and those of Tagore. Gandhi is
a great man working for peace. Do you have a film industry
in India?" The gentle and searching, almost detached eyes of
De Mille looked at me. I told him how impressed I was by
the hospitality everywhere.

"Of course, Mr. de Mille, you do realise that if it were not
for India, America would never have been discovered?"

He looked surprised. "That's a new one on me. How did
you figure that one out?"

"You see," I went on, "Columbus set sail from Europe to
reach India and her wealth and gold, and instead . . . found
America!"

I once wrote him: "You've done enough Western films of
every size and theme. Why don't you be the first to do, as
only you can, something of the East, something from my
country?"

"I am over seventy . . . and I don't plan that far ahead . . .
but . . ." he wrote back.

I am looking forward to his *The Ten Commandments*, his
latest film. The world of America, and the rest of mankind,
may well heed the message of *The Ten Commandments*. Buddha
spoke them five hundred years before Christ, and then way
down to the present age the odd voice has warned mankind.

On a warm, beautiful evening in March of 1938 I went to
the hill-top home of that socialite and charming hostess, Mrs.
Bernadine Szold Fritz. And it was here that I met Max Reinhardt. Intense eyes, short stature, but power emanating from
him.

"I would like one day to do a play with you . . . Indian subject . . . your sensitive face," and so we talked. I also met Adrian, who had dreamed up Garbo's fantastic dresses in her pictures; Janet Gaynor, that tender heroine of *Seventh Heaven*. And Alice Terry . . . I had never forgotten her sensitive and startling beauty in *The Four Horsemen of the Apocalypse*. And sitting in a far corner, quietly, unobtrusively . . . the lady in grey, with a strange peaked hat . . . I was introduced to her by my hostess. "Mercedes, this is Ram." And that was how Pandora's Box of the magic screen opened to me . . . and many new threads, all gleaming and shining started off a chain reaction of influence in my life. . . .

I also had delightful dinners afterwards in the home of Adrian, whose house was filled with antiques and carpets, and lit like a technicolor picture. And there, one evening, I met Nazimova, the Camille of another day, of the silent screen. She spoke of Natasha Rambova who had a lot to do with her film work, as being the only integrating force and influence in the life of Valentino. "After Natasha and Rudy parted, he disintegrated. Artists need influences, good in-fluences. They need the right minds and the right people to influence them to give of their best." How true those words were. Thinking today, and with more perspective, I wonder to what degree the Roman Emperor, Hadrian would have been inspired to do the great things he did for his country, if it had not been for the love of his ideal, the famous Antinous. Stiller and Garbo . . . what a lot I had heard about his in-fluence on this great actress. He had a vision, a perspective of her genius, and that flame-like quality in the young Garbo's personality. Being detached and interested in the instrument that Garbo was, and developing her genius as an actress, he was able to be impersonal. The fact that she was the most beautiful girl in the world did not touch him. As a woman, so I am often told during my visits in Stockholm, she did not interest him. It was that flame within that he wanted to fan to volcanic life. . . . Poor Vishnu, had Garbo come instead of Mohini, and in her silent way just stood before him as he, that God, sat meditating in his forest hermitage, he certainly would have been seduced by one look alone. Poor Mohini, that mythical goddess, had to dance herself breathless before he was disturbed from his meditations!

As I have already said, it was Rubinstein who was instrumental in getting Sol Hurok interested in a recital of mine, for when I danced some months later after Hollywood at the 46th Street Theatre in New York, it was because of the interest that Rubinstein had shown in me.

"Tonight—First New York Appearance—Ram Gopal," the advertisement read. In the next line was the final concert in Carnegie Hall of Marian Anderson. That was what I read that morning. It all seemed so strange. And this was New York, soaring into the sky. How breath-taking it all was! New York was 'Today', it was 'Now'. The East was 'Yesterday' . . . and all its thousands of years. Later, I found that Europe was the yesterday that influenced today's day. But New York was this very instant, this NOW. And how awed I became of its rhythm and its babble and movement and smell of power and money. But I loved it nevertheless. And then I danced. I danced alone to recorded music. I remember nothing of that recital today, except the shadow of Mercedes near me, driving away to some quiet place for supper after the show.

"I sat next to Martin, and he said he thought you a very great dancer," Mercedes said.

"But who is Martin?" I asked.

"Only one of the leading dance critics. What he says influences the masses."

John Martin, Walter Terry and others were most kind and constructively critical of my performance, given so soon after Shankar, my countryman, had danced there only a short while ago. But Shankar gave them, in the words of one of my American admirers, 'the works'. Translated, this meant sex, girls, instruments and himself, with a large company to carry him through the full two-hour programme. And I had danced alone! Carl Van Vechten, who had written such vivid accounts of the dancing of Pavlova and Duncan, long, long before me wrote of my debut: "Ram Gopal . . . bears us away with him from the untruths of everyday life into the reality of his mystic visions. . . ."

I loved every single instant of my first visit to America. On the night I sailed away, a crescent moon hung low in the sky and the stars were bright. Of course it was Siva, winking at me sleepily from the heavens, telling me that this city was something dreamed up out of his meditations. All these thoughts came in a reverie of sadness and sighing as I saw the silhouette of this city of 'Now' fade into the blue of that sunset.

CHAPTER FIVE

Holiday in Hawaii

EDGAR C. SCHENCK, cultural director of the Honolulu Academy of Arts, Honolulu, Hawaii, had invited
me to appear at the superb theatre where so much was
being done to revive the original and simple Hawaiian Dance.
I had been ill, but I could not possibly let the audience go
without giving them a glimpse of the dances of India. Here
I was to learn something of what they had in their art and
culture, and I was also to show them perhaps the original
source of their arts, particularly the dance. Their native
dances use certain gestures of the hands for depicting stories
of myth and legend. I would show them how we told stories
in India with our *abhinaya*, our wonderful gesture language.
But I was ill. How often since, during a tour, with all its
complicated arrangements and travelling discomforts and
fatigues, a dancer falls short of 'perfect vitality'. Well, this
was one of those rare, but not uncommon things that has
happened to me since, then as now. Thank goodness, not
too often! I could not possibly let that audience who had
filled the theatre, go without giving them a glimpse of my
art.

"You tell Mr. Schenck that I'll dance, whatever happens.

And you just tell that doctor that he'll have to give me more medicine and less advice about not dancing. Because if he does not do it, I shall dance just the same, and if anything happens both of you will be to blame," I said rather impatiently to my manager and good friend, Janta.

"But hadn't you better rest, Ram? Then a few days later you can dance. . . ."

"That's silly. They've paid to see me dance and nothing will stop me."

That was how I gave one of several dance recitals in January of 1938 in Honolulu, at the Academy of Arts and Dillingham Hall, where I had had some very interesting reactions from the public.

"There was no attempt made by the artist to be spectacular or dramatic. One's emotions were stirred and stimulated by movements in which there was co-ordination of every muscle of his body, trained by rigorous rules in the ancient dance form of India. Each dance was a series of pictures that originated from stone sculpture and religious rituals. The Cosmic Dance of the God Siva, a gorgeous ending to the programme, portrayed the eternal drama of the Universe—creating, maintaining and destroying it in a dynamic dance in a world of nature that is inert till Siva willed it alive. One felt the pulsing, flowing waves of rhythm—and then came rest as Gopal posed in the likeness of the Siva Figure . . . he has absolute control over his emotions. He is able to portray the serenity of wisdom and age as well as the lighter feelings. Here, dance music formed a united whole. Out of East India has come a star who will undoubtedly take the mainland (America) and Europe by storm—he is faultless."

That was from one of the leading papers of the Islands, and

reading this over mouthfuls of grapefruit and pineapple for breakfast, the fruit turned to nectar in my mouth. The date was January 20th, 1938. So my efforts to dance, in spite of illness, had not been in vain!

". . . Much of the charm of the temple dancer's success is due to his seeming distraction. He seems not aware of his audience—he is within the temple worshipping at the shrine of his Gods. One will remember his calm expression, the flowing flexibility of his hands and arms—all the result of vigorous training. Like the work of a painter in oils, his art is three dimensional—the dances possess visual, audible and intellectual beauty. He essays, and most successfully, to bring to the mind of his audience a graphic picture of the poetic conceptions. Subtlety, fine distinction and precision of detail characterise every movement. Facial expression, the flicker of an eyebrow, twitching of lips, movements of sensitive toes all contribute as much to the illusion as movement of graceful limbs . . . the recital was a rare experience in a form of art seldom seen in these parts. . . ."

Those few extracts by learned critics well versed in the half-way house that Hawaii is between America and the East did much to encourage me. And I was very happy. I saw much of the ancient stone gods of the Islands in the superb Art collections of the local museums . . . walked in strange valleys, heard strange tales of the gods and how, when they got angry, they set hurtling into the air volcanic ash, and lava dripped down, foaming at the sides. I was enchanted . . . everywhere there was a spirit of laughter and gaiety. How 'eternally' happy you Islanders are—so I thought, and I was right. But a few years later, the gods were angry, or in combat, for came Pearl Harbor, and that beautiful land was stilled in tears and defence. But that is how I have found all life, symbolically the eternal process of evolution. It is like the Continual Dance of Siva: Creation, Preservation, Destruction. At the end, rebirth of new forms. "Nothing is new but Forms" . . . says an old Sanskrit proverb.

Of course I had to study the Hula. I did not find this difficult. The movement, as my expert teacher taught it reminded me of both the Tanjore style, and of Manipuri executed in a slow motion of fluid movement. "There must never be a break from one movement into another. It must flow. . . ." How true of that dance and all real dancing.

The Islanders lived with much happiness with their friends the Americans. I thought of the British in India and wondered why we could not live like these two peoples lived, laughed and worked together?

If I had thought that we in India were hospitable to the foreigner, and that the Japanese people were kindly, I had not yet known the peoples of Hawaii. They were full of the most amazing hospitality I had known till then.

Some days later, to the music of an Hawaiian orchestra playing their welcoming and departing songs, and heavily garlanded with '*leis*' I left for America.

"Throw your garlands into the water before you sail out far from the mainland. That means you'll return" . . . shouted one of several dozens of my friends who had come to wave me good-bye. I pulled off garland after garland of scented jasmine, marigold and other varieties, and flung them hastily away. Soon the little party of waving friends dimmed. It was like looking at a group from the wrong end of a telescope, dimmed because my eyes were veiled with a mist.

CHAPTER SIX

Triumph in Warsaw

THE plaintive music of a band drifted in through the port-hole of my cabin. I had a feeling that the music, sad and melancholy, was flavoured and salted with something of the sadness of Indian music. In a few moments, I went on deck. My friend Janta and 'Mamushka', his mother, were there. They seemed still and quiet. I joined them softly. I noticed that they both had tears in their eyes. I thought: 'Perhaps that is how one feels when one comes back to the sacred soil of one's birth. This is Poland. They are carefree, happy and have joy in their hearts.' Then, Janta said almost apologetically: "Don't expect anything as big or as prosperous-looking as the great city of New York. We are such a little country. Nothing like big wonderful America. But Ramciu, we are happy."

Mamushka was thinking that perhaps I would scoff at the small, comparatively poor Poland in contrast to the blinding power and glamour of New York and America. How little she knew or guessed what was in my heart.

"Mamushka, you must remember that India is a sad country, too. One day we *will* be free, and then we shall start to build up our country. But we are sad, too. So you need not worry.

Ram Gopal as Siva, God of the Dance

Ram Gopal as Siva, the Hunter

(*photo: Baron*)

Ram Gopal with Retna Mohini-Cartier Bresson

For you see I feel that here at least there is peace and sincerity, and love and art." I felt depressed. The band had gone on playing that sad melody. It was a melancholy Slav march that was supposed to welcome those on board to Poland. I could not drive away the gloom and foreboding that seized my whole being. I was disturbed. Premonition? Perhaps.

Thomas Janta, the younger brother of my friend Alexander, was waiting in a car. We were soon speeding down those strange forests full of the scent of pine and fir. The road was not very even. After a journey that contrasted so vividly in my mind the difference to America and Japan, I could not help feeling that, because of its very simplicity and wildness, the fir trees and pine forests held a strange haunting sadness, and a gloomy attraction of their own. I had had a subconscious 'feeling' for the land ever since I heard my sister, Flo, a superb amateur pianist, play the tragic music of Chopin's etudes and nocturnes, for to me they breathed the very life of what I was then only intuitively feeling and finally knew to be true.

We went up the driveway, curving up to a large mansion with a little peasant village on its left, a farm on its right. This was the ancestral home of the Janta Polczynskis.

The following weeks were for me the happiest days of springs I have ever known. The cold breath of winter had just begun to leave the sun to warm the land to life. It was my first experience of a European spring! And it was Poland. And I loved it. One never forgets the 'first' of any experience, and this was breath-taking. For it was a land which I had already felt I could 'speak with'. There is something eloquent about those dark, mysterious glades and pine forests. There was that same unseen but strongly felt presence of brooding and invisible spirits.

What a ritual meals were in that beautiful historic home.

F

For tea, there was the steaming Samovar, an assortment of various types of sausages and salty bread which I like better than any other, tea and lemon. I shall never forget the dinners in that large, candle-lit dining-room and the freshly prepared and cooked Polish dishes! I have always loved Polish and Russian food; it has something of both the East and the West. Early in the mornings I used to run alone to an orchard at the end of the garden, and lying flat on the ground, bite the succulent strawberries without even touching them with my hands. I got mud in my hair, but strawberries in my mouth. I had a glorious time shaking the purple plums out of those loaded trees, and how I ate them! I have never tasted sweeter fruit anywhere in Europe before or since. The apple trees I had seen in South India were like rose bushes compared to the enormous apple trees growing here. I revelled in this wonderful spring, and its gifts from the heart of the soil, so rich and varied with its assortment of honey-sweet fruit. Then the garden spirits waved the lilac bushes alive and the intoxicating perfume of white, blue and amethyst lilac filled my every breath with an air of exaltation.

I noticed, too, that the Poles loved to celebrate. There was a harvest festival of thanks for the golden corn, songs and dances and violin-playing, and some very spirited and vigorous dances, so like the pictures I had seen before my visit. With it all there was the great hospitality and love that Mamushka, Janta, and the family showed me in every possible way. I was like some long lost relation coming home. And being still a boy, this made a great impression that has remained in my heart. I belonged among them. They loved me, liked me. I was as happy as one could possibly be.

It was this same beautiful estate that so many Polish noblemen and women from the neighbouring homes came to visit in the evening, for drinks, dinner and cards. To me everything was new, something out of the fairy-tale books. How else could I think of those candle-lit nights, with all those blazing log fires and that warm spirit of friendship that lit all those spring evenings! And was it not to this very estate that my beautiful friend, Mercedes de Acosta, would come, as she did later, and what laughter we shared boating on the streams, rivers and lakes.

"I have arranged a tour of the principal cities for you. I think it ought to go down well. Not very long seasons any-where, but since you are solo, four or perhaps five perform-ances a week, and, in a little while, you'll have danced in all the principal cities of my country," Janta said one day at tea.

"My country is so far away," I replied, "and they know so little about it. They are surely not going to take a solo per-formance, and for a whole evening, are they, Olo?" Olo was his nickname, which Mamushka had used so effectively, I thought.

"My people, all Polish people, love Art, and they are sensitive, and your art is sensitive. So you must work hard and dance the way you do. I'll bet they will love it and adore you."

And that was how I found myself, trembling, in the wings of the great Opera House in Warsaw. Dancing alone. Dancing to recorded music in that same theatre where Nijinsky and Pavlova had danced, once upon a time, long ago. The critics were, I thought, so very generous in what they said about me. It was, however, the article by Professor Tadeus Zielinski that got nearest to what I had tried, and still try to do in my dance. In an article called 'Euripides and Ram Gopal' Tadeus Zielinski wrote in 1938:

"I am writing under the recent impression made upon me by a dancer, who is supposed to be the second of a pair, and it is probably the first time that he has been compared with the other one. This impression of mine was very strong, all the more as it was unexpected. For, frankly speaking, I went to the performance at the Grand Theatre with very modest pretensions, if not reluctantly. Will exotic dances be able to fill a whole evening? Let us hope it will be a nice rest after a day of hard work. Unpretentious, yet better than a bridge party.

"But . . . I walked home absorbed in thought. For I had to admit that thanks to this Indian dancer, Terpsichore's art had revealed to me its secret, or rather a part of it which I did not know yet. The first part of Terpsichore's secret was revealed to me many, many years ago by a once famous and now almost forgotten dancer—Isidora Duncan, whom I could not help comparing with the object of my experience tonight.

"Yes, I spell it, 'Isidora' and though I will probably be called a pedant, I should like to prove why I write this name 'Isidora' and not 'Isadora' or 'Ajsadora' it is because the name means 'Gift of Isis'. I saw Isidora Duncan before the First World War in St. Petersburg; as far as I remember she was to dance at the Komisarzewski Theatre, and her impresario asked me to give, before the performance, a lecture about her which should last half an hour. We agreed to twenty minutes and as it turned out it was just five minutes too long.

"I was severely criticised in the press and one article ran as follows: 'Why all this talk about antiquity? What is Iphigenia to us? You had better show us this little barefoot dancer as soon as possible, that is the only thing that matters!' That is not true at all, and if really a part of the audience thinks so, well let them read their papers meanwhile: the lights in the audience-room are on.

"But you who are interested, please listen. You are going to see the last feminine character which Euripides has created—Iphigenia. She is in ecstasy and offers her

life on the altar of Artemis, because she knows that in her
virginal hand she holds success, victory and fame for her
father, the leader of the Hellenes and the whole of Hellas.
You will understand the pride in her words to the chorus:

> 'Behold—all of Iliou
> I am the Conqueror!'

"This very moment is worthy of a whole life! But—is she
really the last character? Perhaps not. Why—at the same
time as 'Iphigenia' came the 'Bachantes' the real tragedy of
ecstasy. The 'Bachantes' have found their musical expression in Beethoven's Seventh Symphony. In a few
moments Miss Duncan will perform, or rather personify
Iphigenia's ecstasy.

"The Pallas Triology? Yes, because in all these three
tragedies, the Greek Goddess Pallas takes the embittered
and angry poet, Apollo, so to say, by the hand and leads
him to the God who was the protector of his early youth.
And—behold, the fruit of the conversion is 'Yon', the
youth of the temple. (Yon is not so much a creation of
Euripides than of Sophocles from whom Euripides took
the idea).

"At the beginning of the tragedy, the God Hermes, as
the 'Prologue', explains to the audience Yon's fortunes:
This quite in the spirit of the Greek tragedy, where sur-
prises are not appreciated. Then Yon himself appears; he
greets the rising Sun with a prayer, sprinkles water from
the sacred fountain of Castala on the floor of Apollo's
house, drives out the birds who soil the sacred place; then,
bowing deeply to the God, he says: 'Sun of Lato, be
blessed! May I never fail in thus serving Phoebus!'

"And that, yes just that, is what we have seen on the
stage of our great Theatre. It was 'Arati', the prayer of

the Youth of the Temple; he greets the Supreme Divinity, sprinkles the effigies of the Gods with water from the Ganges, and finally in profound devotion prostrates himself before the altar.

"It was but one moment, but it revealed much to me: for, at this moment the Indian dancer turned, for me, into Yon. More than that, he became Euripides returning after long years of distress, to the God who protected him in the days of his youth. David, Michael, Saul's daughter (and one of David's wives) looked through a window and saw King David leaping and dancing before the Lord and she despised him in her heart. 'How glorious,' she says, 'was the King of Israel uncovering himself in the eyes of the handmaids of his servants as one of the vain fellows shamelessly uncovereth himself?' Therefore, no child was ever born to Michael, Saul's daughter, unto the day of her death . . . and, watching tonight the different performances of the Indian dancer, and connecting him with the characters from Euripides, may I be allowed to exclaim with a sort of melancholy: All that really should belong to us!"

I have quoted at length because I think that this critic conveys best the spirit of my dances. Everywhere I went in Poland I visited the shrine of Our Lady. Every time I lit a candle to her. I could talk to her and confide in her and ask for guidance and above all, thank this Mother of the world from the silences and prayers of my heart. The sacred silences of those ancient Catholic churches always lent power and peace to my thoughts and prayers. Long, long ago those sad childhood tunes, played in the dusk and evenings by my sister, time and time again, had etched themselves into my memory and my subconscious, and the more I saw of Poland and the more I saw of her people and her churches, the more

I understood her. What a strange link music is with that of the heart. And when my heart was touched, recollection overcame me, making yet another land that became part of my heart and life.

I remember making a pilgrimage to the childhood house of Chopin. How touching that experience was. I saw the first instrument he ever played with his boyish hands, the house from whose actual windows he had looked out, the trees, the garden. I saw too the matured and tortured death masks of him which reposed like shells of his tormented spirit that, giving beauty through the sadness of his genius, in music, had been crucified by illness and gathered again unto his Maker. I was deeply moved by the peaceful atmosphere everywhere. I thanked a kind Providence that the usual guide was not there to shatter the eloquent silences that filled the stilled quiet of that little house in a garden. I touched reverently the very same notes of that instrument over which his hands had played. How lucky I was to be able, as an Indian, to understand completely the classic storehouse of European and Indian music. The piano, violin, symphony concerts . . . the veena, flute, sanai . . . the echoing voices of the Indian half, and the great compositions of Bach, Beethoven and Mozart with those of the Spanish and Italian composers all invoked within me a visualised and great movement, a world movement of one rhythm, one voice and oneness with all mankind. For music to me is like religion, only unlike the 'practised stunt' of so many self-styled religious priests, either of the East or the West, music was able to enter by the ear and then seep through into the soul and still one into a consciousness of Truth. "Be still and know that I am God" . . . yes, music stilled me then, and, I am happy to say, stills me now.

Each nation has a particular gift and talent, and in Poland everywhere I was moved by the beautiful shrines and historical monuments. After the last war devastated that great country I met many Poles. In all of them burns a melancholy sadness to return to the 'Mother Soil'. In 1944, when I was in India I could well understand the plight of the refugees seeking shelter in India. And still later, when I returned to England, I met many of my old friends from Poland, some of whom were going on to America.

"I want so much to see my mother, just to know she is there and that I cannot go to her or reach her is what tortures me and fills my heart with sorrow," said a Polish friend of mine, Serafin Kycia.

"But you will see her one day soon . . . provided you pray and believe that you will. This is an age of miracles you know, Serafin," I answered.

"But I want to see her now and hold her in my arms. Its worse than death, this torture of knowing that she lives, and yet that we cannot meet. But I will pray and wait and believe in God . . . it is all that one has left, what else is there?"

My young friend Serafin loved the friendship he had been given in England and later America during a visit there with me in 1954. "To think that the Americans were wonderful to me . . . they gave me a visa for one year, longer if I wanted," he said, filled with gratitude, "for I do know that if I wanted to, there was the freedom to go to that great country. But I am so thankful for living and working in England . . . I count my blessings." Serafin's attitude is that of so many other Poles.

After my mother died, years later, I knew exactly what the sorrow of parting from one's mother means, for generally, is she not the most loved of all men born, whatever their nationality, creed or race?

CHAPTER SEVEN

Paris

AFTER the rest and invigorating holiday at Mamushka's country estate, which I was sad to leave, Janta and I set out for Paris. Mercedes had written me from Hollywood that she would try and be there at the same time as I.

"Paris will rub some of its magic off on you. I shall be your guide and introduce you to the right people, whose minds and arts and talents in literature, painting and music, will make you realise that Paris is the greatest of all western cities for its culture and beauty. See you soon. . . ."

The Polish train was pulling me out of the brooding forests, those silent pines and birch-fringed lakes, and the fields and rivers and forests which I had grown to love. It was sundown. The sun had turned a deep crimson; it was a pastel fire, though not quite as red as over the Ganges in Benaras. Somehow I felt heavy at heart, leaving a country that had given me so much love and warmth of welcome. It turned to night. We were approaching Warsaw. Looking out of the compartment window I saw large beams and shafts of light searching the sky. Not one, but several. They seemed to be looking for something. I thought of the Grauman's Chinese

Theatre Film premièr I had seen recently in Hollywood where such lights lit the theatre, the stars, and milling hysterical crowds.

"What is that, Janta? Why those lights?" I asked.

"Oh, just the usual manœuvres, they're trying to spot an aeroplane high up. And all those lights with their powerful beams, will focus on the plane they're looking for. Don't look alarmed. It's just practice," he added, calmly continuing to read some Polish paper.

But I was alarmed . . . something within me told me things were going to be uneasy for this sad and lovable land of which I had grown so fond. Practice? The train crawled into the big station in Warsaw.

"Stay the evening at an hotel and catch the train for Paris first thing in the morning." Paris? Would it be like all those pictures Father had shown me? As beautiful as the colour pictures I had seen in the movies at so many cinemas the world over? I held my breath. And here I was in an express train that would go literally non-stop, hissing and pounding along those tracks at, I was told, something like eighty miles an hour. I wished it could be a hundred, a thousand miles an hour. I could not wait. I was impatient for, after all, I knew that Paris is the centre of the world's beauty.

I dozed off, dreaming of trees, flowers, perfume, a city of beautiful women, where the streets were lined with wine, paintings, and shops filled with everything one could want. I awoke to a roaring sound. It was Paris, a glorious, bright, blue-skied spring morning early in 1938. Here were porters, taxis and people all rushing about as madly as they do in India, I thought. All screaming and shouting and gesticulating. . . . It was wonderful. People looked at you with bright, smiling eyes . . . and the women on the boulevards looked to me, that first spring morning, 'different', and certainly happier than those in the other countries I had just seen.

Paris in spring! There is nothing like it anywhere. It was unbelievable. Instinctively I felt something good must surely happen to me. If I had this intuitive reaction to this gloriously beautiful city, its people must love me and react in the same way.

I remember we lived in a very cheap hotel, not far from the caressing trees whose branches bowed over the embankment into the Seine, with their green leaves touching the water. My room was cosy and warm, and colourfully papered. Soon I ate my first croissant and coffee. This was in the sunlight, and with every woman and poodle looking at me as though they had been expecting me, and with such a kindness in their eyes . . . warm and friendly. And that was how the first morning began. Janta went off, looking up friends, business associates and the like.

"Don't get lost. And if you do . . . well take a taxi to this address," he said, handing me the card of the little hotel at which we were staying.

Alone, I felt a sense of exultation. I walked all the way to Nôtre Dame. Why? Because I had never forgotten Lon Chaney playing Quasimodo in *The Hunchback of Nôtre Dame*. Also, it was a sacred place. And because I wanted to light candles to Our Lady, the Mother, for protecting me and bringing me to so much beauty and wonder in this world. It had all been due to my prayers to Her and to Him. And thanks was something I was always brought up to offer. How I gasped at the Nôtre Dame, and with what awed silence I gazed ceilingwards and saw the most incredibly beautiful stained-glass windows I had ever seen or hope to see. . . and then, walking down quietly to the part dedicated to the 'Immaculate One', I knelt down and thanked Her and lit three candles.

I was out, going as fast as my feet would walk, glad to have said 'thanks' to Her. And straight from there, I went in a

taxi to the Arc de Triomphe. The French priests in that
school in far-away Bangalore had told me that Napoleon had
marched down the most beautiful street in the world—the
Champs Élysées. And it was all the wonderful things I had
dreamed it was, only my dreams were not beautiful enough
and my heart not large enough to contain all that Paris meant
to me on that first day. We had a bottle of wine and a meal
under a pink sunshade on a cobbled side-street. How good
the food smelt and tasted!

Later, I went straight to the Musée Guimet . . . I had to
see the Gods and Goddesses of India, Tibet and China, and
besides, I was told in Warsaw that this museum had lectures
and even a performance of my dances was possible. I remembered reading, in connection with Garbo's picture *Mata Hari*
that this remarkable spy had danced there her version of
Hindu Temple Dances . . . would I dance there too? Possibly.

That night I fell asleep with peace and harmony in my
heart. I felt I was at home. And that was how, like countless spirits before me, I loved Paris on my first exciting day.

We went, in the following days, to the Louvre. I had to
see if the Mona Lisa was really as mystifying as she had looked
in reproductions. I looked long and thoughtfully and I am
still mystified. I had read the tragic story, which filled me
with sadness, about the model who posed for Ingres's 'La
Source', so along I went to see that, and of course the Venus
de Milo. I kept thinking of the nude torsos of the Malabar
women whose figures and breasts I thought were far, far more
beautiful, than the Venus de Milo's. How very masculine
the Venus was. Looking at her face I could easily have mis-
taken her for a man. To me she suggested Power more than
Feminine Beauty as I know it in my country. I started laughing, not very rudely, just laughing.

My friend said to me: "Why do you laugh? One moment
you stand transfixed, gazing at the mysterious Mona Lisa, you

look tragically at the picture of 'La Source', and then you come to stand before this marble masterpiece of Greek art and you laugh . . . you are silly; there may be someone watching and then they will think, 'How silly this boy is, perhaps he doesn't know better.' Do behave yourself!" And there stood my friend more shocked than ever as I continued to laugh. "Will you stop it?" he said sternly.

"Oh, don't be silly; I was thinking about her missing arms . . ." I said, trying to control myself.

"What is there in that thought to make you hysterical?" he countered.

"Well, you see I know you'll think I am mad, but I was thinking of . . . well . . . Mae West. You see I read in some movie magazine that an American sculptress made a marble or carving or something of the fabulous Mae. You know what she replied when viewing her nude form in marble? 'Same dimensions as the Venus, sure. But I've got it on her. I've got two arms and I know how to use them. Besides, dearie, I'm not marble!'"

My friend froze.

"Look, if you want to look like a block of Polish stone," I said, "you can go to the devil. If you've lost your sense of humour, I haven't. Besides, I think I prefer to go and look at everything myself. I don't need your chaperoning." I walked quickly away as anger mounted within me.

I was to go again, many, many times, to the Louvre. Every time there was something of greater perfection at which to wonder. But I did learn that to see Art, one had to take it very, very slowly, assimilate all the thoughts the great painters had at the time of carving or painting their master-pieces.

Which city in the whole world has more 'fountains' of beauty than Paris? I visited and 'drank' in the Tuilleries, the Rodin masterpieces of modern art, which filled me with

erotic wonder and desire, and the Bois de Bolougne. But how
can one list all the places that are centres of learning in Paris!
To me, every tree, every cobbled and worn stone, and every
wall, church and street, the palaces and boulevards, were a
'frozen and silent' testimony and sermon reminding my spirit
of beauty and art and truth.

And then came 'Alba', as I grew to call Mercedes de Acosta.
Fresh from America, she was all excitement and enthusiasm.

"I must introduce you to Madame Sert. And of course
Gertrude Stein. You remember Carl Van Vechten spoke to
us in New York and told me that I was to be certain and
introduce you to her. And then, of course, we will go to the
theatres, the museums and oh . . . well everything, darling.
What memories this city holds for me! Do you know?" . . .
Here she would carry me away with her on a magic carpet
and tell me about Duse and Bernhardt, and the Russian Ballet
of Serge Diaghilev, about the great courtesans and personalities she knew in girlhood and knew now, as a full-fledged
beauty, the like of which I had not yet seen.

From day to day, and week to week, I met the most outstanding personalities in the Arts, Letters and the Theatre.
And then came the invitation for me to appear at the Musée
Guimet. I was going to dance there early in November in
1938. "Danses de l'Inde, par Ram Gopal," read the invitation card for the Association Français.

This museum was crammed full of some of the most rare
Tibetan 'thankas', hanging tapestries, Palava and Chola
Bronzes from South India, and the most fantastic sculptures
from Cambodia, Siam, and wonderful life-size and larger
than life-size Hindu heads of Buddha, the Enlightened One!
That, and the superb reproduction paintings of the Life of
the Great One, painted in life-size, after the fashion of the
frescoes and murals of antique monasteries and temples, in
India and Ceylon, all made a fantastic background. In one

room, right on top, in the library I think, was the Great
Golden Buddha. Here, that evening, I danced to what I was
later told was the most élite gathering of people in the world
of literature, the theatre, painting, music and the dance!

It was a bare lecture platform, no drapes, no lights. A
short resumé of my programme was given by the Curator of
the Museum, Mr. Stern, who described the symbolism and
antiquity of the Hindu dance.

The powers of those gods must have helped me and given
rhythm and fire to every movement of my body, my hands
and expressions, for the critics were very enthusiastic the
next day—and during the weeks and months that followed.
What I liked most about their criticism was the fact that the
most observant and impartial writers, not slavishly addicted
to any national style of one particular Western or Eastern
mode of dancing, had stressed the fact that I had created
images and incidents, and above all the beauty of nature, with
just the illusory images my dance figures invoked, without
the use of elaborate décor, *corps de ballet*, and the usual fifty-
piece orchestra. I could not quite realise then, as I do now,
exactly how great their compliment was.

After my recital at the Musée Guimet, Serge Lifar wrote in
The Figaro on December 13th, 1938:

"A new priest of the dance has come to us from antique
Asia, from that mysterious and enchanting India. The
exotic side of his dancing charms and fascinates us, but
what really moves us is the mystic spirit which animates
him. Ram Gopal leads us in his path into the sacred world
of symbols, that quality so typical of Hindu dancing, and
these symbols arouse in us that sentiment, half effaced
through the centuries, which trace back to a common
source from a country where all Indo-European humanity
was born."

The most hospitable and warm friends, from aristocrats to artists of all nationalities, extended the hand of friendship to me. Preobajenska was teaching at a studio, the Salle Wacker I think, with her tireless little Russian body imparting an art that for Europe seemed very old, a few young hundred years! How young a tradition compared to Indian art! But what industry, discipline and perfection she demanded, and got from those lucky enough to work under her.

Princess Krasinsky Kshesinskaya, the 'prima ballerina asoluta' of the Russian and Czarist patronised ballet, showed me around her studio, studded with photos of world-famous dancers. I watched, hypnotised, as she demonstrated to some students how to dance a variation, her arms, face, neck and feet moving like twinkling stars, swaying to the music of her arms, which in turn framed a face that was pure poetry of expression as she moved. She stopped, and I could have begged her to go on. She said: "Now they dance . . . but too much it is the body, it is the counting, it is the muscles. The feeling is very rare now . . . to see in the dancers. The spirit sleeps. And without the spirit, the soul, it is not dancing. No feeling. Ah well, perhaps in a hundred years they will learn . . . we will all learn, one life is such a little time. . . ."

Such a little time? This legendary figure who first invited and danced with the young Nijinsky . . . who treasured and exchanged 'presents' which she spoke to me about. . . .

"And now I eat. You come? Yes? You eat too, no? Then you sit, drink some red wine. . . ." Quick and swift in her movements she sat down at her midday meal. I drank wine and marvelled at her. "Your dancing, wonderfully fine, noble, you would have grand success in Russia, people there love feeling and soul. You are great artist, I see you dance every time."

Some days later I sent a scarlet Benaras silk scarf with gold lotus flowers embroidered on it to this 'Goddess Parvati' of

Ancient N. Indian miniature of the God Krishna's Ras Leela dance

Rehearsing with Mrinalini Sarabhai at Bangalore

With Shevanti and a pupil in Bangalore 1945

The author's living-room

the Russian ballet, with a note of thanks and adoration. Boris
Kniaseff, my friend, and one time husband of Spessiva, took
it to her. In return, I got a picture with an autograph and
dedication from this great personality and artist. I was told
how she had once been the richest woman of her time. Now
she was comparatively poor, without her emeralds and rubies
and estates. But I thought she was richer—she had the
Dance.

There was a *Gala de Dance* given at the Louvre for Nijinsky.
Serge Lifar had organised it. The funds were to make
Nijinsky's life easier. Since then I have learnt that no artist
ever has an 'easy' life, never, not even till the end. The gala
was held at the Palais du Louvre in the Rue de Rivoli. The
walls were hung with décors that Serge Diaghilev had used in
some of his ballets. Nemtchinova, the Russian ballerina,
danced in her classical and pure style: there were Teresina
and Escudero making the stage reverberate with the rhythm
of the Spanish dance; also Lifar, looking like a Greek God,
and Anton Dolin. I was a little awed, dancing among so many
strange people! But I was thrilled. They were friendly and
warm to me. It was my first experience of 'galas'. And
dancing in the Louvre was an experience in itself!

I was asked to appear at the Gaieté Lyrique some time after
my initial appearance in Paris, and it was this successful
appearance that gave me courage to sign a contract to appear
the following year, 1939, with a company. I was only just
beginning to learn about life and a company and the theatre.
I learned the hard way. But my most valuable lessons about
companies and dancers awaited me in India. Not when I
returned in the year 1939, but later during the war. However, of that later.

Mercedes de Acosta and I had had so many talks. "This
evening you'll come to the studio of Gertrude Stein. You've
heard about her. Carl Van Vechten showed you her photo in

New York. She has been to the recitals you've given and liked your dancing so much, in fact, that she had made me promise I'd bring you to the studio.

"Gertrude, here is Ram. . . ." Timidly I looked into a very strong face with two bright, strong, penetrating eyes.

"Your dancing moved me the way Duncan's did, in quite a different way, but the effect was the same." I was dumbfounded. I tried to say something. I could not. A strong hand held my arm and she said: "Now come, what will you drink? There is fresh lemon juice. Oh, this is Alice Toklas, my friend. Get him an orange juice. Of course you are Hindu. Vegetarian? And you don't drink, do you?"

In a few strong, powerful strides, like some moving rock-hewn image, filled with life, she said: "Look there"—pointing to a wall—"you see that girl with flowers?"

"Yes," I whispered.

"Well, that is a Picasso," she went on. She showed me other still life pictures and others all hung in her studio house; there were so many of them!

Frankly, I was not moved. They lacked 'soul' for me. Technique, yes. And obviously painted by masters . . . but masters of composition and style. I had the same feeling as when I watch a purely technical dancer perform: it left me without emotion. And how absurd they looked in my memory after what I had seen in the Louvre and Frick Gallery in New York.

"You like them . . . don't worry, I know you're moved . . . he's a very great painter . . . and I am glad to have helped him . . . of course his style is unusual. . . ." And so she went on. "I like your very ancient poetry. I've read some but not all of it. It's too complicated. But now and again the fables of the 'Panchatantra' have made me laugh. You know why your civilisation has survived? Because the Wise Ones knew how to laugh."

Later we relaxed, sitting down after walking through her art collection of Picasso's painting. Then she became human. The great, imposing, strong face lit up with kindliness.

"Carl wrote to me about you. . . ."

And she suddenly seemed withdrawn and you could almost hear her shut her doors of 'contact'. We chatted for a while. Alice Toklas spoke with Mercedes about something or the other. Then the Great Lady carried on, this time in a different vein, about exhibitions of contemporary artists, painters whose works held promise. I carried away an impression that she was a Wise One. "A rose is a rose is a rose. . . ."

Retna Mohini, with whom I had become friendly, and who desired very much to join me in India, decided that she would follow later. She would be my partner. She showed me some of her Javanese and Balinese dances. She was like an ivory figure moving with exquisite grace, and had the most unusual face that reminded me of the Fish-Eyed Goddess of Madura. She was married to a young French photographer, Henri Cartier-Bresson, who has since become world famous.

One day, Mercedes De Acosta said to me: "Ram, I feel restless . . . some feeling of uneasiness, restlessness . . . I don't know what it is. I've written a wonderful script on Joan of Arc, and I do wish Greta Garbo will play it one day with her artistry. You know, the more I see of life, the longer I live, the more convinced I am of the inner life. Everything is so outward in the West. Surely the ancient ones, who lived the Inward Life, found something that the great saints of the West seemed to have savoured of . . . peace and strength. I am strongly pulled to India . . . I think I'll go and see the Sage of Arunachala—Maharishi."

"Of course you must go, Alba. This is the *Kali Yuga*, the Black Age. The age when the machine carries man . . . faster I think than is good for him . . . for I feel that today nobody seems to know where they want to go. But everybody moves on faster and faster . . . and where to? Yes, go, and if you feel the inner restlessness and hunger for India, follow your instincts and go as soon as you are able."

We parted. I returned to India. My friend Janta came later. I arrived back home alone. On that boat, I realised that Janta had a narrow vision of life. He had taste too, and sincerity, and great talent with his writing. He was a good friend. But there was something lacking in his friendship with me. The more I talked of the early influence of my 'pull' towards things of the spirit, of religion, the harder he urged me to turn to his way of thinking and life, which rather alarmed and sometimes confused me. But perhaps, after all, that 'somewhere' between the elevated planes of Yoga, Mercedes De Acosta's search for Truth, and Janta and his sensual outlook on life, the Truth *could* possibly be found. But I could not figure out in what manner, and in what way, and certainly not now. But that did not stop me looking, and thinking, and finding out first hand. If I did fall flat on my face trying to find out, at least the Wise Ones would not blame me. They would say I was trying, attempting and reaching for some grains of Truth. And what harm was there in that?

CHAPTER EIGHT

Return to India

I HAD no idea what sort of welcome, if any, would greet me in my own country. After all, I had set out with just a box full of costumes and some specially made records, unlike Uday Shankar, whose large company of musicians and dancers were all trained by himself in his own creative and personal style, which was quite different from the pure classicism of Kunju Kurup's Kathakali dancing. Yet when he returned to India I remember that the press and public alike had gone wild over his triumphs abroad. It filled every Indian with a sense of national pride in welcoming this great creative artist. And what would happen to me?

I had not long to wait. We docked in Bombay, and there in all the wonderful heat and blue skies of an Indian morning I stepped off the boat. How different India looked that morning, and what perspective travelling the world over had given me. But it was wonderful to be back home on one's own earth. Waiting for me was a group of friends; a much larger group than I had expected. And what a warm, loving greeting they gave me.

"There is a small gathering of press journalists and photographers. They are so eager to know your reactions, not to

Europe and America, great as they are. But they want to know about the Far East. You see, Ram, you are the first Hindu dancer ever to have danced in Burma, Java, Malaya, the Phillipines, China, Japan and Hawaii. Now that's a great record. Well, come on, tell them how the Far East reacted to your dancing . . . well, tell them anything." I was taken aback. A small gathering indeed! There, sitting before me were a few dozen journalists and what would I tell them?

"Did you find the Far East interested in the art and culture of India, the Motherland?" asked one. Before I could reply, another asked: "Is there any colour bar against Indians in New York and America? How about Paris and the French?" "Are you tired?" "Are you happy to be home again?" "Did you like the Japanese girls, or prefer the beauties of Fifth Avenue and Paris?" And so on. I was certainly being scrutinised.

They could see that I was very young. Clumsy in fact, at handling them, nervous in replying to the great avalanche of questions that kept sweeping in on me. But I could see that their intentions and interest were kindly. Further they were friendly. I answered in the best way I could. One of my friends said at last, after what seemed an age: "And now let's have something to drink, gentlemen. . . ." Thank God. It was over. News of my success abroad had certainly been relayed regularly to the press in India. I was grateful for that. For they should know how seriously I had tried to interpret an aspect of our art.

"So now you are world famous! Are you sure it is your dancing that the public liked, or was it your beautiful body, Ramji?" asked one.

"Look," I said, "you find out for yourself. Before I return to Europe, I shall dance in Bombay, and when you watch the audience's reaction first hand I'll ask you that question. How about that?" Laughing, I said good-bye.

Shortly after my arrival, Retna Mohini, Cartier Bresson and

Janta joined me at my home in Bangalore. What a home-coming awaited me! Nothing elaborate. Just simple. It was more from the expressions in my mother's eyes, and the voice of my father, that I knew that they were happy I was home again, and pleased—perhaps even a little proud. Without any delay I said: "And now I will dance for all of you and some friends."

Retna Mohini and myself wasted no time. A short while later found us both working hard at the Kerala Mandalam near Shoranur. Ravunni Menon, Kunju Nair and the Poet Vall-athol, all welcomed us. Janta joined us a few days later. How we worked! Ravunni Menon was only interested in teaching Retna, my partner, those portions of the Kathakali dance that were soft, graceful, feminine, the *lasya* style as he called it. And Retna learned fast. With her extraordinarily pliant and supple body, trained in the strict and hard school of the Javanese dance, Retna found that she could quickly master these *lasya*, or feminine movements Ravunni Menon and Kunju Nair were taking pains to impart to her. Naturally we sat up many nights during our term there, watching the all-night Kathakali dance dramas. Retna was carried away by the power and dynamism of these dramas.

"Oh, Ram," she would say to me, "if some of these dances could be shown in the West, the audience would go wild about them, they are fantastic, unreal, unbelievable. I have never seen such virile and powerful dances. Of course, with Ravunni Menon, most powerful of the teachers, it is quite understandable. Oh, my San"—her nickname for me— "thank goodness I am not one of his male pupils. He kills them with work. But how powerful and violent their movements are!" How right she was. This task master in the strictest sense of the word drove his male pupils to hysteria on occasions, but how they learnt to dance! One day we watched him take a girls' class.

How friendly Vallathol became with Retna! He made signs with his hands and face, being the expert that he was with his *mudras*, and Retna understood all he said by his gestures alone, as she did not know the Malayalam dialect. As he spoke, gesticulating excitedly, Retna would listen attentively, her large fish eyes glued to his face and hands; her head would nod like an echo of his own, and she would somehow communicate to him that she understood. They were like two dumb people making signs at each other. Knowing how very eloquent Retna was, I could not help laughing at the changing expressions on her face as she 'listened' to his *mudras* and expressions.

Janta took many pictures of the school, the all-night dance dramas, of Vallathol, Retna and myself, and the great gurus who were teaching there for that term. Unfortunately, when war came to Poland he lost many of these valuable negatives. Fortunately Retna had hidden a few in Paris, and these remain as interesting documents of that term we had there learning more fully of the ancient tradition of Kathakali dancing. John Gadsby, enthused by the accounts I had written him from time to time, decided to spend a holiday in India, and joined us at this school in Shoranur.

I created many duets and solo dances for both Retna and myself. We used the Kathakali dance technique, and gestures and rhythms. But the dances were strictly creative. I had seen how beautifully the traditional Kathakali dancer, Madhavan, trained in the strict style of this school, had used the technique for helping Uday Shankar create his ballets and solos and duets—a style that embraced both the masculine and feminine aspects of this great dance tradition. What a superb dancer Madhavan was, for both he and Gopinath, the Palace dancer of Travancore, had thrilled me with their great artistry. All Europe and America had gone wild about Madhavan, whom Shankar had discovered and whose company was thereby greatly enriched. I believe he married the daughter of my guru, Kunju Kurup and lives today in South India. It would be a pity if the public in India did not see more of this brilliant dancer's work again.

"I have had replies from Bombay, Delhi . . . and guess what? The Globe Theatre in Bangalore," Janta told Retna and me, as we finished eating a simple meal off a banana leaf.

"When do we dance?" came the simultaneous reply from both Retna and myself.

"As soon as you and your costumes and musicians are ready," he replied.

After thanking our gurus, Vallathol and other members of this great institution, we left for Bangalore. There we had our premier of the second All-India Tour. My first acquaintance with the public had been with that other American dancer, La Meri. One evening in March 1939, we danced at the Globe Theatre. Let Fred Harvey, an Englishman, the organiser of the Theosophical Art Group in Bangalore, tell you what impressions he had of this performance:

"That our local lad has made good is sure to be the unanimous and enthusiastic opinion of all Bangaloreans who have had the privilege and pleasure of viewing Ram Gopal's wonderful performance at the Globe Theatre. I had previously seen Ram Gopal dancing, but before he left Bangalore for his world tour; on his recent return at which time he gave private dance recitals for the entertainment of a few friends, I was much impressed, but I was very curious to see how he 'came across' the footlights. On seeing him the other night at his public performance, I was more than satisfied, and I am greatly of the opinion that what he is giving easily surpasses anything on these lines which we have had before in Bangalore.

"I was charmed with the general get up of the show

from the rich black velvet stage draperies, the unique head-dresses, the gorgeously beautiful costumes of the dancers with their beautiful colour contrasts to the simple but effective white Bengali dress of the musicians, and the interesting musical instruments.

"The collection of dance items were all admirable, each one perfect and polished, as a separate stone on a costly string of pearls, but I felt that the 'Garuda' The Golden Eagle, was remarkable for its spectacular effect: the Krishna and Radha Duet Dance excellent for its exquisite grace and fluid movement (a poem in motion), while the temple *puja* item was as delicately and austerely appealing to the senses as are moonbeams seen in a forest glade. The three dancers are all excellent in their particular parts, either when performing separately or together. The balance of acting is kept very even. There is no sub-ordinating or exulting of any individual player. Each is allowed to do his or her part without any cramping or over-emphasis, and the result is perfection.

"The Javanese lady, Retna Mohini, gives the effect of grace and rhythm, so easy and effortless are her movements. . . . But Ram Gopal is outstandingly unique. His perfect body, his strikingly beautiful features, the manner in which he can express himself by movement or glance, his knowledge of the technique of the Oriental dance, his clever footwork, the strange effect of tallness he has when on the stage, the way in which he enters into the character he is portraying, or the emotion he is expressing, all combine the ensemble that we can only express by saying: 'This is Ram Gopal the dancer.' I feel sure that Ram Gopal and his troupe of dancers will be a bigger sensation than ever on the forthcoming world tour, and I wish them all the luck they so truly deserve."

That write-up, coming from Fred Harvey who had seen my initial struggles as a youngster, years before, in Bangalore, was indeed a tribute. In a way I think that it also summed up the good will and pride that the citizens of my home town felt for me.

We moved on to Delhi. We were announced to appear at the Regal Theatre in the heart of that capital. When the curtain went up, there was a big black yawning gap of empty seats, row upon row! I was shocked. Retna was stunned. Janta was speechless. But the show must go on, and it did, to a practically empty house. There were several reasons for this disastrous failure in Delhi, the main one being that the public were not aware of the performance for lack of publicity, and secondly, that the season for dancing there was the wrong one, as the resident Viceroy was not there at that particular time. Whatever the reasons, Retna and myself danced just the same, and just as if the house were full, as they had been in my home town.

Her great sense of humour came to the rescue. "I koch a cold, San-San," she said to me.

"You caught a what?" I asked.

"I koch a cold, I koch a cold," she would say hopping around on one leg like a Javanese clown. How we laughed when she said how she 'koched her colds'. She meant the draught in the theatre was so cold that it 'koched her'!

We came finally to Bombay and appeared at the Regal Theatre. Here the public response was so great that we were asked to extend our season. The houses had been enthusiastic in sharp contrast to the damp response we got in Delhi. How grateful we were for this response. Unfortunately, we could not extend that season, or accept several other offers that came pouring in from different parts of India. There were those contracts to fulfil in Europe. I returned to Bangalore, gathered some more instruments, costumes and other personal belongings, and after a tearful good-bye to my parents, we left for the West.

"And remember, whatever happens, don't forget to pray," added my mother to me.

Then slowly, that small, tiny train crawled out of the station. We were on our way to Bombay to catch *The Viceroy of India* steamship to Marseilles. Arriving at Bombay, with our small band of artists, both dancers and musicians, confident that we would have a great success in Europe after our appearances and the audiences' reactions in three major cities of India, we sailed. But not before I had gone to offer thanks to my secret Shrines, where a White Goddess, called Mary, smiled benignly.

India disappeared in the mists of a pale sunset. This boat was a fast one, reputed to be the fastest on the Eastern routes. The sea looked deep blue that evening, and was calm, and again that night, hanging with one eye half awake, was the Crescent Moon. Of course it was the God Siva. I remembered the way he hung so brightly that night I left New York, and here I was going again, leaving my homeland. It was an omen. I felt that my little band of artists would have a success in Paris and London. That was the happiest voyage on a ship which I had ever spent, when I come to think of it. It was sad to leave my home and my beloved parents, but I had to be grateful that I had this chance of dancing again in the West. Going up the Suez Canal, into the Red Sea, and then out into the blue dreamy Mediterranean, how I loved every minute of this exciting journey.

We landed in Marseilles, and then entrained immediately for Paris. Would Paris give me the same thrill and excitement I had experienced that first time, again? I would soon find out.

It was April in Paris. The sun shone brightly, and a shower of perfumed rain fell the morning I arrived. Sunshine and rain at the same time! In India some believe that Gods are celebrating in the heavens when this happens! But whatever they were doing in heaven, I was certainly having a thrill on earth in this most beautiful of European cities on that April morning.

"Come, John, let's take a taxi and drive instead to the Bois; the luggage can go on to the hotel by itself. It will be all right, please . . ." I pleaded, and John Gadsby, who had accompanied me on that voyage, agreed. We drove straight to the Bois. I stopped the taxi and I remember running out and greeting the first buds and early green leaves of spring. How good it was, arriving in Paris when it was spring. It was spring and summer and autumn the year before, and now it was spring again. I determined to work harder than I had ever done. Retna and myself had our bulging notebooks of new dances in our own peculiar notation that every dancer has, unintelligible to all, but the dancers themselves.

The next few weeks were occupied with morning and afternoon reharsals at the Salle Pleyel. Janta, who had become a good business manager, had told me that Eugene Grunberg, the impresario, was very enthusiastic about the wide field and possibilities that lay open to our ballet. He was arranging a season in Paris. How would Paris like the group I had assembled since my previous appearance there last year? Would the public and the critics like it as much as my solo performances the year before? I would soon find out. Of one thing I felt confident, that with my live musicians I could have a far greater scope to do what I wanted than dancing to that authentic but nevertheless 'canned' music.

And there one comes to a problem. How difficult it is for authentic Indian dancers going abroad to take a fair-sized company and give recitals without any guaranteed period of work. Expenses are heavy, and the risk of such a venture can only be taken against odds. That was what I thought then, with reservations; that is what I believe now more firmly from past experience! However, anybody taking to the art of dancing, and going around with a troupe, has to be slightly mad, for when measuring up the difficulties that one is liable to encounter, and the hard work against returns, it is not worth the effort and trouble. For the impresario, in most cases, sits back and makes the profits while the artists slave. Art is indeed a labour of love.

There was very sad news in the papers one evening in Paris. That beautiful city was deeply moved by the victims of the submarine *Phoenix* which had sunk to the bottom of the sea, owing to some mishap to its engines, and everyone had been drowned. The families were left destitute, and I was asked whether I would perform at the Salle Pleyel for this worthy charity. I readily consented. The performance raised quite a sum for the victims' families, and the reviews of the critics were wonderful, and I had danced again for the great public of Paris, where I hope to have the same honour many, many times again.

CHAPTER NINE

London

I ARRIVED in London for the first time one wet, cold, foggy spring day in 1939. How sad and desolate everything looked; so different from Paris, I thought. I felt uneasy and unhappy. I had arrived to make my début at the Aldwych Theatre in the Strand, and had carelessly forgotten to pack my little lucky charm, my 'remover of obstacles'—Ganesa, the little Elephant God I had always carried with me.

"Either you get my Elephant by plane, or I leave immediately for Paris. I couldn't dance in this great strange city without him. I would never be a success. Besides I don't see how you can be so optimistic; why should they like Indian dancing?" I said to John Gadsby. I was depressed and I sounded that way.

"Well, Ram, I'll certainly telephone your hotel in Paris and you'll get your Elephant by all means. But come on, snap out of it. The London public are sure to like you. What makes you sound so gloomy?" asked my manager.

"Oh, I don't know. I am not so certain . . . somehow. . . . Oh, well never mind. Do you think the weather is going to be like this all the time?"

Sensing that that was what depressed me, Gadsby replied:

"Well, the weather here is pretty awful. Very unpredictable
. . . but don't worry, I am sure it will change tomorrow.
However, take some rest to soothe your nerves. A good
night's rest, and tomorrow the sun will shine for you, I
promise," he said smiling.

Oddly enough, the next morning the sun did shine. It was
as bright as Paris. Instead of arriving at the theatre at nine
that morning, I decided to leave my hotel and drive around
the parks, and look at the Palace and take my first glimpse of
London. What an experience that was! It did not captivate
me immediately like Paris. Instead, I was impressed with the
solidness of everything. Hyde Park looked like a Turner
landscape, with the willows 'weeping over the Serpentine,'
and when the taxi drove along the Embankment, I realised
how important it was for all great cities to have water
running through them. It purified everything, cleansed
everything. London was impregnated by the spirit of Man;
Paris, that of Woman. After getting my first glimpse of the
Palace and Marlborough House, the car sped along towards
Trafalgar Square and up the Strand, past India House, to the
Aldwych stage door.

It was a strenuous day, with the reporters, press, rehearsals
of lights and costumes, but when I sat down to dinner that
night in a quiet flat in Pall Mall, which a friend had rented
for me, I felt less depressed than the day before. I realised
that London did not 'embrace' one with its atmosphere and
spirit the way Paris did.

As the evening approached, I felt terribly nervous. What
would the people say, and how would the critics like my
dancing? Surely this thought must be the most recurrent one
to occupy the dancer! Since, I have been told of two very
famous ballerinas, one English, the other Continental, who
sit back and devour every word the critics say about them
from their bedside scrapbooks. Vain? I do not think so. It

serves as a stimulant to try and do better next time. Do not authors, however famous, do the same when their book reviews come out? And painters? I felt that even Shakespeare must have often read and enjoyed and been amused by what a lot of people said about his works. And I thought again. Would the press and public alike understand this remote art of Indian dancing?

The curtain went up and I danced. There was a 'House Full' sign outside the theatre. By the time my turn came to perform, which was about a quarter of an hour after the curtain had gone up, I was filled with terror. I could not possibly dance. I would forget everything. But I danced!

I remember nothing more from that moment. Certainly the applause was great, and hundreds flocked backstage.

Lord Lloyd, who was Governor in some part of India—Bengal I think—sent for me shortly after my first appearance. I arrived one afternoon at his office. "My wife and I were in India for several years. But I have never seen anything like your interpretation of Hindu dancing. . . . I must say we intend coming often during your season here. I really wanted to see you because Her Majesty, Queen Mary, who is very interested in things Indian, would like me to take you along to Marlborough House for tea. Wednesday afternoon? Would that be all right?"

"Of course, I am honoured. Yes, Wednesday afternoon."

And then I met Queen Mary. Lord Lloyd walked a little ahead of me, leading the way. "This way, sir, please," said a gracious lady-in-waiting.

We were led into a warm, carpeted room, and through the windows I could see a beautifully kept garden. The whole atmosphere of the place had a magic about it that was hard to describe. Everything carried an air of individual elegance. But what impressed me most was the great taste and individual arrangement of every single item of furniture

H

and the antique cases that filled this ancient house. Of course only a Queen could live in so perfect a place. But to me Queen Mary was more than just that. Her spirit went far beyond the confines of being a Queen; it reached out and touched beauty in everything that was created and fashioned by the world's greatest craftsmen and artists. And the atmosphere? One could feel her presence everywhere. I had the feeling that it was similar to something I felt on a summer's day in Kashmir, many summers ago, when I first caught a glimpse of the Himalayas. It was grandeur. And all these feelings came upon my young mind before being ushered into the actual presence of Her Majesty.

"She is human and warm and kindly . . ." Lord Lloyd said to me. But even though he said it, I thought he looked a little flushed in the face and certainly was exerting all of his English control and detachment to look calm and quiet. The air was charged with an electric expectancy.

Another gracious lady-in-waiting, this time a silver-haired person, nodded to us. We followed. And there, standing by a table in her reception-room was Queen Mary, her hand extended in greeting. Lord Lloyd greeted her very shakily, followed by me. For a moment I forgot whether to do as he had instructed me or to curtsy like a débutante! I was nervous and pale with awe. After she had taken her seat, we both sat down and tea was served. There was, in spite of everything, an air of simplicity about her, and perhaps it was that that made one feel so awed by her very presence.

"It was the most colourful Durbar I have ever been through," she said, referring to her coronation in Delhi. "We were very generously entertained by the Maharajas there. The picture I had of Northern India is something that I carry in my memory as the most beautiful and touching that I have ever known. We saw many pageants, but I don't think I remember having seen any dancing, certainly not the sort my friend here tells me you are going to show us."

The hovering ladies-in-waiting emerged like white moths from the background and we were given more tea and offered more delicacies. There is a lot in the old belief that good things taste better when eaten off the finest made porcelain. But tasty as were those cakes, it was that great spirit that sat before me, embodied as one of the great Queens of history, that drew my attention.

"I may come and see you at the Aldwych. Do you like ballet, Russian ballet, I mean? De Basil's ballet is appearing here. I have not yet seen it."

She beckoned to one of the white shadows that always hovered around, who noiselessly, lovingly came forward at her bidding. Queen Mary turned her head in profile and spoke to the lady-in-waiting. I did not hear what she said. I looked instead at her profile. It was not Grecian, or even Roman, but there was a certain line and curve of beauty in it that had the strength of Rodin's 'The Kiss'. The female figure's head is turned upwards. And there was that wonderful cluster of pearls that clung closely to her neck. Aphrodite! that is who she reminded me of, the Mother of Aphrodite! And that immaculately groomed silver hair which shone like platinum, with a slight blue tint in it. Her eyes were a penetrating grey-green.

Presently, the hovering spirit returned, holding in its hands a silver satin programme.

"This is a souvenir programme of the Gala given to us on the Coronation of my husband, the late King George V. Look at the pictures," she went on. "We are not likely ever again to see anything approaching that Gala."

Slowly turning these pages, Lord Lloyd and I glimpsed into another day and age, an age of elegance, in manners, dress and taste. The programme notes contained the title of one of the ballets *Le Pavillon d'Armide*, I remember the names of some opera singers who were at the top of their glory at the time. But it was that fading gold lettering of the name of Nijinsky that caught my eye. There were, I remember, Karsavina and Cecchetti too.

"I said to King George, as we entered the Royal Box that the whole of Covent Garden looked more like something in India. All your Maharajas were there, blazing with jewels and gold and their maharanis in *saris*. My husband remarked to me that the artists who were to perform that night would certainly have a great feat to perform in equalling the splendour that scintillated below and around us. Nothing has equalled that Gala since. . . ."

She gazed out of the window at the garden. Her expression convinced me that she was recollecting across that span, how times had since changed. All that disappearing aristocracy; perhaps there would never be such a collection of titled people from the East and the West as was gathered together that night for the Gala Coronation.

"Ballet is a very arduous profession. But my friend here tells me that your dancing exceeds the training required for the ballet. It takes seven or eight years to be proficient in your style? Has it anything to do with *Yoga*?"

"Yes, Your Majesty . . ." and briefly, I outlined what the authentic Hindu dancer attempted to convey.

"I have a collection of some antiques that may interest you. A few pieces of jade and jewellery. . . ." She was sitting like Isis, the Egyptian Goddess, absolutely erect. Never once did she slump or lose that poise or balance. And the grace of her gloved hands, the manner in which that neck held the head, with the expression of stern kindliness and sparkle in her incredibly beautiful, glowing eyes, were something that I could not help noticing as a dancer. When she rose from her seat, there was no hurried motion, no moment of awkwardness; she rose as gracefully as she had been sitting. She rose like a cloud going up to a peak. It was breath-taking. I remember, too, the subtle perfume that clung around her. It was something of an English wood, filled with lilies of the valley, lavender and rose . . . and yet it was her aura that impregnated and charged the whole atmosphere around her with that of a queen. When she walked, with us following, I noticed that her heels were not very high. A Swan Queen, I thought.

The antiques turned out to be a priceless collection, gathered over a period, that only one who had known the best could afford. I could not attempt to describe them. Shortly after our privileged view of one of the world's greatest collections by one of the world's greatest women of the twentieth century, or any other century, we departed.

That afternoon, when I danced, I was suffused with the emanation of this wonderful Queen whose dignity, with its kindliness and royalty blended into my dance. I have never seen her like, anywhere in this world. But since then, as a great admirer of this great lady, I have never failed to go often, both before and after the war, to the museum in Kensington, at the far end of Hyde Park, and gaze into the glass cases, and see all the beautiful creations specially made for her. Her dress, her bags, her shoes and even the fans she used. How great a tribute it was for that other great Queen, Pavlova, Queen of the Dance, to have a small glass case allotted to her with her White Swan costume there for all to see. Of the many ballet dancers I have met, I find that few, if any, had even heard of this dedication to Pavlova, and of those who have, even fewer have cared to pay a visit to see it!

I met many interesting people in London, but after the Queen most of the other English personalities I met seemed an anti-climax. It was after meeting her that I realised what duty meant and service and suffering. The words 'dedication' and 'royalty' became synonymous to me. My art took on a greater sense of dedication than I had ever felt before; since then I have, from a distance, admired and loved the great service and love that the British Royal Family give to their Empire. However hard a ballet dancer of Eastern or Western style may work, or for that matter, a Welsh coal miner, it must still take nerves of steel to combat the varying and complicated system of service demanded of royalty. That this great institution has survived only goes to prove how well disciplined, selfless and utterly devoted they are to the ideals to which the British Nation so ardently clings. I feel from that lesson alone, the whole world and every individual watching royalty, both on the newsreels and perhaps in person, can learn to smile and serve; for however dark the times or however bright, that service and those smiles, like the smile and selfless service of the present Queen Mother, must inevitably turn the darkest moments into glory and success. Queen Mary and the Royal Family ever remain to me the symbols of everything that is elevating, dedicated and selfless. They are what the great wise masters and sages of India would call 'Enlightened Karma Yogins' which means 'Enlightened Spirits of Destiny'.

During my performances at this time every evening two artists sat like ghosts in the wings, one on the right side of the stage, the other on the left. The one on the right was a young English artist, Kay Ambrose, who did some amazing sketches of ballet dancers in action and had illustrated the books of Arnold Haskell. She was an artist in pen and ink, of the ballet and its life. The other? Alexander Janta had taken me to have lunch with a countryman of his, a Pole, who was introduced to me as Felix Topolski. This great artist was uncanny in capturing the very spirit of the times, situations and people, whether from the streets or among the Members of Parliament. Felix did some sketches of me which are unique. We have become very good friends since, and I am one of his greatest admirers. A *News Chronicle* supplement carried an interesting sketch made by Topoloski. The article is amusing; it read:

East is East

"And West is West, and never the Twain shall meet," sang Slogger Kipling, who evidently knew little of the London tailoring trade, to begin with. But his axiom would seem to fit the situation Topolski has depicted snugly enough.

"Lithe, brown, graceful, weaving delicate arabesques or assuming hieratic poses pregnant with hidden symbolism, the dancer Ram Gopal brings to the London stage the enigmatic and disturbing East. Under his feet the lotus springs from the dusty boards. Behind him the painted canvas and batons dissolve and vanish into the dusky blue magic of the night, in which strange Gods walk and brood, many-armed and Elephant-headed, to the throb of strings and drums and soft pipes discoursing elusive music, clear and cool and translucent as water dropping from a jungle spring. . . ."

"Ram, read this and this and this," my excited manager had told me. "And you remember you liked the books of Haskell, Arnold Haskell, the English critic?" He was more excited than I was.

"Oh yes, I remember. I like the way he writes about these great artists of the ballet. Why? What has he said?" I enquired.

"Don't be silly, he has not said anything. He has written you a letter, read it."

It was a very enthusiastic letter and enclosed within it was the following notice he was posting to some ballet magazine:

"I pretend to no knowledge of Eastern dancing. In this case it is not necessary. Whatever the tradition, it is obvious that Ram Gopal is a great artist and as such his appeal is universal. He has technique, beauty, subtlety and with it all an extreme simplicity in his relations with his audience. Rarest gift of all, when alone on the stage, he is able to make us visualise a whole frieze, a Living Ajanta.

"I repeat, I do not understand Eastern dancing: Ram Gopal gave me exquisite pleasure as he must to all who love the dance of whatever tradition. . . ."—Arnold Haskell.

"You see, Ram, that is very high praise from so distinguished a critic. Aren't you happy?" His face searched my eyes for an expression.

"Don't get so excited. I am not happy. I am grateful, deeply grateful, for this praise," I added.

"Mr. Gopal, with his unearthly physical control, his lithe remote, yet ominous grace, held the audience transfixed. . . . Mr. Uday Shankar introduced us to Indian dancing, but it must be admitted that, ungrateful though it may seem, he has been surpassed. Mr. Gopal's art is so inspired and so finished that it is as if one were observing the dances of Siva and Krishna themselves. . . ."

This was in the *New Statesman*. The notice was handed to me by Janta. "It's the most important literary paper and to get that . . ." he exclaimed. "Well, God knows, you've worked for it. Perhaps you deserve it. If only the public knew what you have suffered and been through in your Far East travels and the way you were left penniless in Tokyo. Yet they rave about your dancing. How much of an artist's sufferings does any public ever see or remotely guess, I wonder? When Pavlova danced in Tokyo, I remember, how often she would break down crying . . . the tensions, the strain of dancing and the heavy demands made upon her. And here you are, young and with your life ahead of you. . . . I wonder if I would say that you were lucky?" He looked grave.

"You sound as if war were declared and you were pronouncing some terrible prediction," I said. "Personally, I am grateful for all this. But I know exactly what I am putting in and what I have been through. Whatever happens, at least I can say that I have been lucky to get all the experience that God has given me in exchange for whatever I have suffered," I quickly replied.

An artist needs a great deal of encouragement and constructive criticism, and being the giver, has to know how the public reacts. Dynely Hussey added to my pleasure when I read another distinguished paper which is read by most of the literary and scholarly of the vast public in London. . . .

"Ram Gopal's wonderful supple body, his sensuous arms and athletic grace all combine to make his dances as Siva, fierce creator and destroyer, Indra fingering his flute and Garuda the great Golden Eagle, unforgettable experiences. The Eagle dance, with its realisation in human movements of the flight of a bird, made Mlle. Riabouchinska's 'Golden Cockerel' seem for all its brilliant execution a mere child's imitation. Yet in none of these things—the flute playing, the love making or the bird movements—is there anything approaching realism. The real has been translated into the terms of a highly conventional, sophisticated and stylised language of movement."

I met Markova backstage during this season. She was in black and reminded me of Pavlova. "Do you try hard to look like her?" I asked.

"I don't try. I do look like Pavlova. That's the way I always looked. You see, I was the youngest English girl in Diaghilev's ballet. And I have worked so hard always. Always will. But after Pavlova's death I made a promise to myself to try and dance like her, be like her, and devote all of myself to the ballet. And you, Ram Gopal? Are you pleased with your success here? What rave notices! You should be pleased. I love reading my notices. Over and over again. If they admitted it, all dancers, all artists and I am sure politicians also, love reading what they, the public, or the papers say, think and write about them. You are pleased?" Alicia smiled.

"Now come on, Alicia," said Anton Dolin, "Ram must be tired after these two performances today. Some day you must come out to Beatrice Lillie's place, Ram. We'll drive over and play tennis. Do you play?" "A little," I replied. "I won a few cups, all junior trophies, of course. It is good relaxation and gets one's thoughts away from the Dance. One needs to get perspective. When can we play?" I asked.

"Tomorrow noon? Will that do? All right, I'll pick you up at your flat in Pall Mall."

The next day Anton Dolin and I played tennis. I remember he played the best he could. He was obviously out of practice. But so was I. "I am going to win this set six-love, Anton. And the next, and the next . . . all six-love . . . and then watch you tease me that you're a champion. And I'll tell everybody I thrashed you," I laughed.

"Don't you dare tell anybody . . . I'll strangle you, Ram. You little devil, you must have been playing tennis as long as you have been dancing!"

That night, Alicia and Pat came again backstage. "We had to come, we love your dancing, admire it so much."

"Alicia, do you wear jewellery?" I asked. "Yes? Well, please take this little souvenir." I took one of those Mysore gold-washed, silver necklaces and put it around her neck. How girlish and shy and utterly happy she looked. She kissed me.

During this tour, there was a dark-skinned girl appearing with us from Old Delhi, called Maya Rani. She was jealous of Retna's success. She said to me, eyes glinting with anger: "Retna has swollen eyes like those of a goldfish. Why don't you tell her to make-up properly?"

"You go tell her yourself," I replied; "besides she looks wonderful from the front of the house. Haven't you read what the press think about her? She is Javanese and she cannot have the eyes or looks of a Hindu."

Like some Javanese Peri emerging from the dark depths backstage, Retna Mohini had heard everything. Calmly and quietly she came forward. I thought we were now to have a scene. I should have known better.

"Maya, I like soooo much your Peacock Dance, such a lovely bird. So vain and colourful. Maya, is it your birthday today? I have a little present for you. I think you like it. You watch me from the wings when I dance, I do the same when you dance. We both see things, we both perhaps have opinions, yes? Here take this," Retna added, and quick as a Javanese clown, she vanished into the blackness of the stage afterwards.

Maya was in tears. Her dark, over-powdered mother consoled her and said: "Retna made a mistake. How could she have given you that Gilette set? It's for a man to shave his moustache and beard. Of course she made a mistake. Don't be silly, come on now, get out of that crying and temperament. . . ."

That night Retna and I laughed as we have seldom laughed before or since. I understood her sly 'passive' humour and always loved her the more for it.

And that briefly summed up the thrill of dancing in

wonderful London town. The privilege of meeting one of the greatest Queens, the joy of reading those critics, and the drama of backstage. Then we left for Paris . . . and more engagements.

CHAPTER TEN

First Impressions of the
Russian Ballet

IT was early in the 1930's, and I was having a holiday with
friends of my father, the family of a rather middle-class
Indian merchant. I was at the house of Enakshi Rama Rao,
a home town friend from Bangalore, famed as much for her
beauty as for being one of the first respectable Indian Society
girls to take to the 'ignoble' art of the cinema.

Enakshi said to me: "Ram, I thought you might be
interested, and perhaps like to visit the Ajanta Studios where
my husband, Bhavnani, is shooting his latest film. There is
going to be a dance sequence of toe dancers, Russian ballet, I
believe. They are a troupe on their way back from Australia,
and I am told there is a great dancer, Olga Spessiva. She is
not dancing in the film sequence, but you may be lucky
enough to meet her, perhaps, and then see what their dance
is like compared to yours. Would you like to go?"

That was how I first saw, at close quarters, Russian ballet.
They were all nymphs in rather bedraggled costumes. I
remember one particular girl, a typical Russian starlet of the
dance, with a severe centre parting in her hair, melancholy
black eyes that sparkled when she danced, and a dark skin.

She seemed to move with grace and ease. It was said by her companions and the *maître de ballet* that she would be a very great star one day. They rehearsed to some ballet music again and again. I noticed the sweat pouring off their bodies and faces in that humid heat of a summer's day in Bombay, under the hissing arc lights. I had no idea what that particular Russian dance number had to do with the film. I was too absorbed in watching the dancers and the strange attitudes they struck when they took up their positions. There were about twenty of them. I remember they drank water and muttered in a strange language that sounded like a mixture of Punjabi and German. There was a distinguished, grey-haired gentleman who never smiled. I kept thinking that he looked like a character played by Erich Von Stroheim in some spy melodrama I had seen—taciturn, unbending and entirely mask-like.

Bhavnani said to me, taking me across the studio floor: "Ram Gopal, this is Mr. Dandre, the great Russian impressario. This is his troupe. This is Ram Gopal, a young boy from Bangalore, home town of my wife."

"Good morning, how do you do? You dance? What dance? Hindu dance? My wife, Pavlova, never saw any dance in India. She went to Madras. You do Temple dance?" And so he went on, stern, and yet in some strange way, kind, but very cold and distant. Asking questions but not waiting for an answer. I remember nervously mumbling something about learning the dances of the south. I was frankly scared and it must have showed. Seeing this, Dandre continued: "Perhaps you come Taj Mahal hotel. There great ballerina Olga practise every afternoon. You come all right, Bhavnani Director arrange everything tomorrow, good-bye." It took my rather awed mind several minutes to understand what he was trying to say or mean. Bhavnani kindly explained later.

A few mornings later, towards noon, I was taken up to a

a ballroom with large mirrors and there, at an improvised *barre*, Spessiva was bending, relaxing, stretching her spine and legs in poses that reminded me of some thin, undernourished Saras preening its rather wilted feathers—a bird like the stork, which one sees on river sand banks in India. She had large black eyes with dark rings around them and a patient, smiling pair of lips, resigned like those of an Indian widow. Her neck betrayed the strain her frame was going through for the art of her dance. What painfully thin arms, bony and skeleton-like! But wonderful thighs and legs, long, slender and pointed in her ballet shoes. To the quick tempo of a pianist, up and down, up and down she went, extending her legs and arms in varying positions. I was told that in a few moments she would be introduced. There was a pause. She met some Indian dignitaries with me, who watching her rehearse were I am sure as puzzled as I as to what on earth she was trying to do with those extraordinary attitudes she was taking, and why so painfully thin a woman strained herself so much in the movements we had witnessed.

"'Ow you do, da . . . da ow you do. . . . Plea's I meet you . . . I lof your *sari* . . . eet ees sotic costume. . . ." She was complimenting one of the Indian ladies who, with me, had been watching this strange woman. "Ah . . . Dandre say you dancer . . . vat dance you do? . . . I like see you dance . . . show me please one day, you very young boy. I am tired . . . this heat too much for me . . . I must practise every day . . . now I dance variation. You watch, please take seat . . . sank you . . . sank you. . . ." And feet turned out like a duck, she quickly moved away to the pianist, and he played some lovely fragments from Chopin or Tchaikowsky, or both, I forget which. And then she danced in her practice costume.

Suddenly she became another woman. Her soul seemed to emerge from every movement and it seemed to me that she smiled and danced with some invisible being with whom she moved with the most exquisite grace. I did not know what her dance meant. I did not know what she tried to dance or convey. There was something rather tragic, childlike, lost and yet, with it all, a quality of 'giving' to me, in her dance, that made me choke. I thought that her points were like shooting stars in the night. And then she stopped, perspiring more than ever.

Later, sipping orange juice, she told me that she had been ill during her recent Australian tour, and that she was going back to dance in Europe . . . she would have liked to see Indian dancing but where did one see it? What was the difference between the street dancing, the courtesan dances and the folk dances? Dandre spoke to her. Then she got up, and wishing us good-bye, wrapped herself delicately, like some flower in tissue paper from a florist's, and moved away. I caught a last glimpse of her as three Spessivas, reflected from the central figure, moving towards a doorway that was flanked by enormous mirrors. All three figures seemed aspects of the one delicate creature that so pathetically walked away. Ghost-like she vanished. I never forgot that picture or that meeting.

My next contact with the world of ballet was from a green-covered book I bought off a station bookstall in Calcutta. The year was 1937. It was marked 'Nijinsky'. From the moment I opened the first few pages of Romola Nijinsky's story of her husband, I was held in a magic world. I loved lingering, long and slowly, very slowly, moving along the wonderful rose gardens of my mother or at the great botanical gardens in my home town, and I lingered because I could not bear to part from the spell and fascination that beauty held over me. The flowers, the perfume, the strange trees and the variety of cacti held a strange power over me. Great music, sad music, to me depicting Nijinsky's early hardships and

(*photo : Angus McBane*)

In traditional Kathakali costume and make-up

(*photo: Angus McBane*)

As a Rajput Warrior in a North Indian Kathak Dance

wanderings in Russia, held exactly that same magic. Slowly, deliberately I came to the end of each page, pondered lovingly over the pictures of Nijinsky and wept at the engulfing doom that robbed the world of Western ballet of its greatest male dancer.

It was very clear from Romola's book about the ballet that the subsidy of the government in Russia allotted to the art of the Dance was big enough to allow artists to dance and study seriously, painters to compose their décors without difficulty, and composers to dream up the most amazing ballet music yet heard. Who, since Tchaikovsky has composed anything comparable to his music for *Swan Lake* or *The Sleeping Beauty*? In contrast to the spiritual quality in certain moments of *Swan Lake*, I have never seen equalled the barbaric fury and spectacle of De Basil's *Scheherazade* and *Prince Igor*. And then one is told so often by balletomanes of the Diaghilev era that De Basil's productions lacked the fire and were comparatively rather pale reflections of the original Diaghilev ballets!

Naturally I went many times to the Diaghilev Exhibition after the war at Forbes House. Room after room was filled with pictures, paintings, photos, sketches, costumes, and above all 'atmosphere' which the organiser, Richard Buckle, had magically captured. This was undoubtedly the greatest exhibition ever held in London to date on the art and design of ballet.

As I walked round the exhibition one day with Tamara Karsavina, the great ballerina of Diaghilev's company, she said to me: "This only shows how impossible it is to comprehend the genius of Diaghilev. It is good to see that so many young companies, springing up in Europe and America, all draw inspiration from what Diaghilev brought across, but they miss the essential point. You see he was interested in Art, and not in the nationality of the ballet company. When

I think now of his head-strong and self-appointed successors it makes me fear for the future of ballet."

This would have sounded very awesome and sad had not my friend, Mercedes De Acosta, who was with us, broken in and said: jovially "Come, Tamara, Truth and Beauty once given never fade, but go on and on, and somewhere, however invisibly, the right time will come and bring the right people and the right circumstances to reincarnate all that glory. There is no time or limitation to Truth and Beauty."

Next I must speak of Pavlova, for she wove her enchantment in India and the Far East as far as Japan, in addition to conquering the entire Western world. As far as the Hindu dance in India was concerned, and I believe she visited India twice, somewhere in the early twenties and towards the end of her career, Pavlova discovered Uday Shankar, and with him created her Radha-Krishna Ballet, urged Menaka, an Indian socialite, to take it up as her life's work, and even got the South Indian Rukmini Devi, the Theosophist, to give up studying Russian ballet and to look for her own dance forms in South India. All three of these pioneers of Hindu dancing in the late twenties, fired by Pavlova's own life, took to dancing.

In my opinion it was Shankar and Shankar alone who surpassed them all, as he still does in his wonderfully creative ballets.

Comolata Banerjee, who wrote the delightful music for Pavlova's ballets in the early twenties, told me what a perfectionist Pavlova was. Nothing 'good enough' would do for her, it had to be the best. She also told me how incredibly Pavlova changed her whole being with the donning of her Indian costume and how she became a living Ajanta Frescoe, and the very incarnation of Radha herself, that she rehearsed non-stop, and how, during her tour in India, while most of the members of her company, which included some virile young male Russian and Polish dancers, gasped for water and lay panting under whirring fans, Pavlova was at the theatre early every morning, gaily, smilingly, happily 'loving every moment' of her India, and practising for hours on end.

Since my first world tours in both the East and the West, how many professional and non-professionals have I met who have told me that it was Pavlova who was the high priestess who initiated them into the art of dancing. Imagine, thirty years ago, somebody carrying the art of a little-known dance style, in tights that exposed so much of her limbs, conquering with her peculiar hypnotic spell, otherwise ignorant audiences. In addition, she herself danced Russian, Japanese, Mexican and Hindu dances.

People today talk about the enigmas of Pavlova's Art, for Pavlova, like Garbo, had something intangible in her personality that made her a being apart. So many people have told me of her personality, prismatic in its iridescent light, and her power seemed to have cast its radiance over not only those out front watching her various characterisations shape and reshape themselves before her eyes, but also those actually on stage with her. As a dancer myself, I have met many oustanding personalities on the stage and screen, and I know how few and rare are those personalities who can enchant me during an actual performance with fellow-artists who know the dark and light side of every outstanding artist, stripped of all illusion.

Douglas Fairbanks showed me a film pieced together of Pavlova doing improvisations of her famous solos, or a selection of her solos on the set of his father's *Thief of Baghdad*. The year I believe was 1924, and I think that much of what I feel in her performance in that roughly shot film, stripped of all the technical tricks of shooting a dance sequence today, is best summed up in what Richard Buckle wrote of her: "What is greatness? What is 'star quality'? I never saw Pavlova—

until last Sunday; then I saw her as close as you are to me, and my word, if I ever doubted it, I don't any more! She was great, great, great! There she sat, large as life, perfectly clear, and for several minutes she mimed 'Christmas', sitting on a sofa. She smiled, flirted with imaginary suitors, slipped out of her cloak, held a rose and cried a little. I saw her tragic neck, her transparent Russian Jewish face, and her eyes brimming over with the Odyssey and the Divinia Comedia and the complete works of Shakespeare. All the things Pater said about the Mona Lisa were true about her. . . ."

Another great artist who has inspired so many is Vaslov Nijinsky, who had danced with Pavlova, and whose death in 1950 came as a tragic and sudden shock. Nijinsky had become part of everything that savoured of the fantastic, mystical, religious and perfect that any living male dancer had ever been or meant to me. And now he was dead! There were stupid headlines that evening in the papers, so full of ridiculous and undignified sensationalism. Reading the news that afternoon, one would have thought that some mythical performing tiger or elephant of Barnum's had suddenly cast its mortal skin and in full view of a 'well informed' press evaporated into thin air. The appalling lack of dignity and the so-called pictures of Nijinsky—mostly they were of his sister and other male dancers in costumes similar to his—to this day fill me with horror at the devastating nonsense and power the press can exercise over the minds of a sensation-loving public.

Nijinsky had once come to see me dancing at the Saville Theatre in 1948. He had never seen Hindu dancing. I was told his wife would be with him and they would be in a box up left from the stage on which I would dance. Can you imagine my thoughts? 1937, that bookstall, those faded green covers, the book by his wife Romola, and now he would be sitting in the box up left from the stage and I would dance for him tonight. It was like dancing for Siva, God of the Dance himself. During the interval, I was led around to meet him, and in spite of having met many outstanding people in both India and the West, I was filled with a sense of awe.

"Please don't look too fixedly at him," Romola, his wife, asked some of the people with me—I think it was an assistant stage manager or impresario, I forget which—"you see this is the first time Vaslav has come out to a theatre, and he seems to have enjoyed the first half very much, and please," looking warningly at some flash-bulb reporters—"no pictures." But for what happened later she might have spoken to the winds, as far as reckoning with those reporters was concerned.

And then I looked at that face—olive complexion, Tibetan Mongolian eyes that slanted towards the temples, a straight nose in profile, rather fleshy in full view, and lips that seemed to be half smiling, half compressed, at some dimension that was not perceptible to me, haunting and childlike, but terrible in its indifference. I cannot say that the face looked either old or young.

While his wife spoke to me, translating my answers and his replies, I detected that he was not quite "gone into the other world" as they said. I had the impression that he radiated kindness and love; his spirit came out and met mine. And the psychic impression that I got was the caress of a wise sage who was sending out thoughts of love and understanding to me, far stronger than the usual meaningless babble of words that are exchanged among people of the theatre. I handed to him from a tray that a waiter had brought in, tea and sultana cake. With quiet composure he extended his beautifully poised hands and I noticed that with the first two fingers and thumb of his right hand he helped himself to the cake. Childlike, pure, crystal clear and simple, his whole face radiated a peace that is hard to define. The elegant manner in which he drank tea made the Woolworth china seem like priceless Czarist porcelain. Every movement of his hands was filled with an elegance and grace which could not escape me. And to think that, wrapped up in a very ordinary tweed overcoat, and plain English-cut suit, he could convey such grace!

Romola smiled kindly and benignly at me. She was patient and loving, like someone carefully tending a magical tree whose flowers bloomed once in every thousand years. Her whole attitude was one of patience, resignation and calm, with a strange Madonna-like look of sadness in her beautiful eyes. I was afraid that I could not agree that she was a negative influence in his life. Many people had many views, some of them not very kind, about her marriage with Nijinsky. But who is anyone to judge the actions of two individuals in a world of free action and thought? And who, anyway, were her critics? They were not the ones who nursed Nijinsky through the veiled years of his retirement as Romola did; and yet so many would make accusations about Romola's lack of this, that and the other, that one would have thought they were first-hand witnesses on that fateful boat which changed the course of life for two of the great characters in the drama that was Diaghilev's Russian ballet in those not so distant, but seemingly far off years.

Nijinsky was interred with the usual ceremony. The crowd departed. I had withdrawn a little distance under a tree. After the throng had disappeared, I approached and threw in a few handfuls of earth and softly laid flowers I had brought for his grave. I said something like this in a whisper: "Good Father in Heaven, take this Child whose body served you, danced for you and broke itself for you in its short span of life on this earth as a dancer; keep him forever where there are eternal melodies for him to dance to, where the rising and setting sun will light the stage where this great Nijinsky will dance for you, and spare him the painful rebirth of ever being incarnated to dance and suffer again on this earth as he did! Beloved friend, gentle-eyed dancer, receive from Ram, who speaks for India and Asia, these flowers, these prayers and these tears of mine, tears of sorrow, and tears of happiness that you have been released from your earthly bonds —receive my prayers and love on your new journey into other worlds."

I walked away, I got into a taxi and drove home. The tragedy of the immortal Rose had filled my heart. That night I dreamt Nijinsky had become a Tibetan monk and that he was happy. I told Romola later about that dream.

Platform 12, Victoria Station. There is dense fog. It is noon. The rear carriage of the train, a wagon for carrying trunks and heavy baggage, lies bare. In its centre is a heavily crated box, within which lies the shroud of Nijinsky's disturbed remains. Madame Legat is beside me. Tears are in her eyes, but she smiles. There are some of her pupils around her, little girls learning the art of ballet. And there in the heavy, wooden crate is the shroud that holds the mortal remains of one of God's most devoted priests, who spoke his sermons through movements, and his benedictions in his expressions and his Love of God through the Dance. That distant red light, half submerged in the steam and fog of the station, dims. I look at it and wonder if the Dying Swan's ruby jewel which Pavlova always wore like a drop of blood on her immaculate white, could have looked as symbolic and tragic as that crimson cyclamen light. Then the red turned to emerald green; I jerked back out of my dreams into the reality of the moment; there was a shrill whistle. With a loud and heartless bang, the porters shut and fastened the doors of this goods wagon. But the pupils and myself had placed some yellow daffodils, flown from sunnier Jersey, on his bier. Slowly the train left the station. Platform Number 12. Nijinsky's remains set to rest in London, now leave London for Paris to lie beside Vestris, a god of the Dance of another day and age. Like some great, disappearing vision, the mists obliterate the last glimpse of an ugly wagon. A station again! It was at a station in Calcutta that I had first bought a book about Nijinsky by his wife in 1937 . . . and this was some time after his death in the fifties. . . . It was London. I was glad again to wave good-bye to him, for the last time, till eternity.

CHAPTER ELEVEN

The War: Pilgrim's Progress

FAR above the skies of Europe, away into infinity, the war god Mars had flung his challenge against the forces of light. The reverberations of this small, insignificant Earth, shook with the destructive aspects of Siva. I could not help thinking of these words from Marcel Schwob writing in *Le Livre de Monelle*:

> "This is the teaching: Destroy, destroy, destroy! Destroy within yourself, destroy yourself, destroy all around you. Make room for your soul and for other souls. Destroy because all creation proceeds from destruction . . . for all building up is done with debris, and nothing in the world is new but shapes. But the shapes must be perpetually destroyed . . . . break every cup from which you drink."

That Great God who performed his Dance of the Setting Sun, Lord Siva, amidst such tranquility, is he not liable to moods of violent energy in his cycleic Dance of Creation, Preservation, Destruction? And the seasons, those glorious colours that come every year in Kashmir, in Hyde Park, Central Park in New York, and the Bois in Paris? I had seen it first hand. First, the early promise of Spring, fresh, bursting, pink and green, flowering into Summer. How warm and filled with promise Summer was. This was the time that farmers the world over clawed and ripped the Earth, of that Great Mother (that Goddess aspect of fruitfulness), tearing her bosom for milk. And her milk flowed in Autumn and gave rich harvest according to the amount of labour put into those who dug deep into her bosom and sowed into it their most fruitful hopes and seeds. Winter was a time when all Nature slept. The old husks were shaken off, cruel as it was, the branches were stripped bare of their tinted foliage, and in Kashmir the lakes froze, and the blinding blaze of Sun reflected on snow told of the deep freeze that was 'recreating' itself for the New Spring, the new life incarnate that awaited, being reborn and reincarnated into the coming Spring. And so the process went on; had gone on from the beginning of Time and would go on till the end of Time—Maha Kala, the Tibetans called him, it was all the same."

This war of Man against Man was perhaps but another aspect of that cycle of evolution that an excited and frightened civilisation called the wrath of Mars. What thoughts assailed my heart as my boat carried me back through that very same blue Mediterranean. Only a few months ago I had sailed through her waters, filled with hope and ambition and desire to impart something of truth and beauty to the world. And there, right in the midst of that success in London and Paris, Mars, the War God, had stirred the heart of Man and he was out to destroy what he could not understand, would not understand. In my mind I saw innumerable churches all over Europe and England ring out to God the Creator to avenge His wrath on the common enemy. I wondered. What would I do if God had asked me to arbitrate? Upon whom would I cast the blame for what was happening in World War Two? I thought of Michael Angelo's wonderful picture of God the Creator, Father of the Universe, painted centuries back. I imagined a great, big, strong hand scratching the face of a powerful brow, the picture I had of God, that of someone not a little amused, but someone watching His own creation getting out of hand. I thought also of that blazing bronze gold statue of Siva which countless devotees worship in that remote temple in Tanjore.

The contrast of Paris with lights, and Paris with her veils of darkness drawn in sorrow, was something that will live for ever in my memory. How atmospheres change! When a city is happy, like human beings, its face glows, carrying you on an invisible stream, and when that same face was sad? Well, one wept with it!

Paris was a woman, a beautiful enchanting woman, whom no man, having seen, could resist. And yet Paris was the name of the man who had been seduced by the Golden Helen of Troy. Then what, really, was Paris? Was it the city where in every aspect of its life the male-female principle, which the ancient ones in India called the duality of *Ardha-Nari* was clearly exemplified? This thought puzzled me. But London was a Man. And New York, that perhaps was the Giant which these two cities had fashioned from their loins and those of various European children that had stemmed from their civilisations.

The ship was carrying me through the Red Sea. Was it true that this sea once parted at the touch of a rod? And it was hot . . . anyway why were these crazy thoughts coming into my mind? Were they crazy? Or were they of any real significance? I could not tell . . . then. How I prayed to that Great Mother for the safety of those I loved, those countries and people and friends whom I was leaving behind, to God alone knows what horrors! Looking to the East, ploughing slowly through the hot Red Sea, I remembered that sometime, in the mists of antiquity, the Sermon on the Mount was preached to a chosen people.

And out of the grief and sadness in my heart for the great civilisation of Europe and the war that was to bring havoc to untold millions, I recalled the story of the 'Bhagavad Gita', or Song Celestial. Arjuna also was in anguish. Strong, heroic and full of action, he had that moment of doubt. Arrayed opposite him were his foes on the battleground of Kuruk-shetra, said to be a site near Delhi. In torment, he asked God whether he should abandon destroying so many human lives to conquer his enemies. And the voice of God speaking through Krishna apparelled as a charioteer answered:

"O Krishna, seeing these my kinsmen gathered here desirous to fight, my limbs fail me, my mouth is parched;

"My body shivers, my hair stands on end, my Gandiva (bow) slips from my hand, my skin is burning.

"O Krishna, neither do I see any good in slaying my own people in this strife. I desire neither Victory, nor Kingdom, nor pleasures.

"Teachers, uncles, sons and grandsons, grandfathers, fathers-in-law, brothers-in-law, besides other kinsmen, for whose sake empire, enjoyment and pleasures are desired, they themselves stand here in battle, forsaking life and wealth. What avail, then, is kingdom, enjoyment or even Life, O Krishna?

"These warriors I do not wish to kill, even though I am killed by them, not even for the dominion over the three worlds, how much less for the sake of this Earth, O Slayer of Madhu."

Speaking thus in the midst of the battlefield, Arjuna sank down on the seat of his war chariot, casting aside his bows and arrows, his mind overwhelmed with sorrow.

The Blessed Lord said:

"O Arjuna, whence comes upon thee in this critical moment this depression unworthy of an Aryan, disgraceful and contrary to the attainment of Heaven?

"O son of Pritha, yield not to unmanliness; it does not befit thee. Casting off this mean faint-heartedness, arise, O Terror of thy Foes!"

Arjuna said:

"With my nature overpowered by pity and depression and mind confused about duty, I implore thee, tell me, O Krishna, with certainty, what is good for me.

"I am thy Disciple, instruct me, who have taken refuge in Thee. For I see not what can remove this grief which withers my senses, even if I should obtain unrivalled and flourishing dominion over the Earth and rulership over the gods."

And the Blessed Lord said:

"As in this body the embodied soul passes through childhood, youth and old age, in the same manner it goes from one body to another: therefore the Wise are never deluded regarding the Soul.

"O mighty among men, he is fit to attain immortality who is serene and not afflicted by these sensations, but is the same in pleasure and pain.

"There is no existence for the unreal and the real can never be non-existent. The seers of Truth know the nature and final ends of both.

"Know that to be indestructible by which all this is pervaded. No one is ever able to destroy that Immutable.

"These bodies are perishable; but the dwellers in these bodies are eternal, indestructible and impenetrable. Therefore fight, O Descendant of Bharata!

"People will ever speak ill of thee: for the esteemed, Dishonour is even worse than Death.

"These great car-warriors will think that thou has withdrawn from the battle through fear. And thou shalt be thought of lightly by those who once honoured thee highly.

"Thine enemies will speak unutterable, disgraceful things against thee and blame thy valour. What can be more painful than this?

"If thou fallest in battle, thou shalt obtain Heaven! If thou conquerest, thou shalt enjoy the earth. Therefore, O son of Kunti, arise and be resolved to fight.

"Regarding alike pleasure and pain, gain and loss, victory and defeat, fight thou the battle. Thus sin will not stain thee."

India was dark in spirit at the raging war that was bursting into flame and disaster all over Europe. Would the whole world perish? Was this the final dissolution spoken about in the ancient texts?

If it had not been for my meeting with Mahatma Gandhi in Bangalore during one of his vacations in Nandi Hills, some thirty miles from Bangalore city itself, I would not have had such a strong pull to the 'inward life'. This meeting lent me so much strength for the constant trials of 'outward life'. But for many impressions and conversations with this great kindly 'Man of the Holy Books' who practised what he preached, I should not have been so convinced and attracted by the occult truths and teachings so beautifully put into the simple verse and language of the 'Bhagavad Gita', the Song Celestial. In my opinion this is the greatest of all Sanskrit literature. To Indians it represents what the New Testament does to the peoples of Europe. I remember how in the afternoon sun of those hazy, health-giving Nandi Hills, Gandhi would sit down, handkerchief sheltering his head from the warm sun, with a group of disciples around him, and read extracts from the 'Bhagavad Gita' and quote extracts from the New Testament.

"You see all truth is One. It is because Man has this incredible sense of 'I am' instead of 'Oneness' that the troubles of the world come in cycle after cycle of distrust and calamity. If only those who read the Holy Scriptures would slowly meditate and dig into the Enlightening Truth concealed within their pages, how much more at peace Man would be with himself."

When he was reading these chapters, his whole being became radiant, his eyes shone and his aura melted the hard crusts that surrounded all of the people sitting beside him, both old and young. I can still see the people gently massaging those slim legs . . . the legs that had carried him all over India, walking into the houses of the poor, into the back streets, into and out of prison. And here he was reminding us to read and hold fast to the Holy Books; the Christian Bible, which he knew so well, was to him of as great a value as the 'Bhagavad Gita'. It is a pity that more Europeans do not read the treasures of Truth concealed in the 'Bhagavad Gita', and more Indians the Bible of God and His commandments. The circle of their knowledge would then, in my opinion, be complete.

I never forgot my first meeting with this 'God and Love intoxicated' Saint. Like Akhnaton or Amenhotep IV, who reigned in Egypt in 1375 to 1358, Gandhi believed in non-violence and the brotherhood of all human and God-created life. Akhnaton's 'Hymn to the Sun' embodied in spirit the same love and goodness that Gandhi's life exemplified.

"I am not a great singer," I remember Gandhi saying one day when he was talking to his group, "Galli Curci and Gigli would laugh if they heard me trying to sing. But come on . . . let us all try, at least the Almighty above knows that it is in the spirit of things that we offer up this Hymn." And in a strange mixture of voices all the various Indians from distant parts of India sang 'Lead Kindly Light'. I thought to

myself that some of the voices sounded comical in their pro-
nunciation of some of the words, quite unlike the way my
elocution teacher would sing them. I had to restrain myself
from laughing out loud sometimes, as one of the followers
from the province of Bombay had the most amusing accent
in some of the lines of this beautiful hymn. But so serious
was the expression on Gandhi's face and so filled with happiness the expression, with his eyes shut as he sang, that I
myself was carried away and sang the song from my heart.

I met Gandhi a few times between 1940 and 1947. I had
danced for him, too. My recollections of this gentle saint
are very vivid. Physically, he was thin. His skin was a golden
brown, clear. He had a shaven head, and wore spectacles
which he had a habit of taking off and wiping. His eyes were
cherry-brown and when they lit up at some amusing incident
could laugh with the generous expression of his large mouth.
When in repose, either praying or deeply engrossed in writing
or reading a letter, Gandhi's face, particularly the eyes, with
half-closed lids, looked as though they had all the sorrow and
sadness of the world laid on them. At moments like these
his face, for me, assumed the grandeur of nature. His hands,
not small but medium, had sensitiveness, and when he
touched you or blessed you with those hands, then you felt a
great feeling of peace come upon you, and on such occasions
the peace that filled one's mind and being was similar to the
mere look of that Sage of Arunachala, Ramana Maharishi of
South India. Personally, I had the same spiritual impact
of peace and spiritual power from both, but the manner
of receiving 'grace' from these two great Masters was
different.

It was Gandhi who said to me: "I do not understand the
Tamil songs of South India. I do not understand what the
Kathakali actor is trying to say with his variety of gestures.
Music, to my ears, is more understandable than the compli-

As the Golden Eagle, Garuda

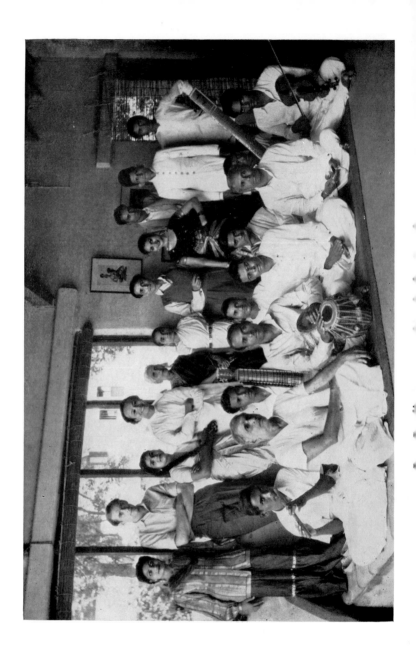

cated gestures of our dances. Why don't you preface each of your dances . . . explain . . . talk to us, tell us what the dance expresses and what it is trying to convey in its spirit. Then we can all enjoy that which we understand much better than this guessing game. . . ."

It was at the Regal Theatre in Delhi that I spoke for the first time to an audience from the stage, because of what he had said. And something that had not occurred to me occupied my thoughts. How many people of the north, Delhi, Baroda, Jaipur who speak a different dialect from those of Madras, Cochin and Trichur in the south, can possibly understand what is being enacted on the stage? In Japan, everybody spoke Japanese, and basically the noble-man and the peasant alike, watching the Kabuki could understand everything because the language was widespread. Possibly in China, too. But here in my country India? How could the dance of the north be understood for both their technical beauty and classical music, when to most people of the southern States of India both were foreign? And it was this very disconcerting thought and difficulty that made me break my steadfast rule that 'Dancers should be seen and not heard'. After that, very often, and not without nervousness, I prefaced my dances with a little talk on what one tried to say in the rich vocabulary of South India's dance idiom.

One of the highlights of my last Indian tour (1946–47) was the recital I gave at Delhi. Among other things, Delhi has always been a city that has fascinated me with its Moghul palaces, old Red Fort and ancient city known as Old Delhi.

One night, my friend Diwan Chamanlall, brought Jawaharlal Nehru backstage at the Regal Theatre during an interval. I remember the great thrill and excitement that the entire troupe got, not to talk of the state of nerves I had worked myself into. To meet one of the great architects of New India, to see him in the flesh, and to talk to him was an

K

honour. The thought that two hours of his life, a very
crowded life filled with innumerable tasks and duties that
needed superhuman strength, should be given to me for me
to show him the pure and beautiful classical dance of India,
was indeed a great privilege.

On being introduced, I could not help noticing the sad
expression of his eyes. Almond-shaped and large, they
seemed to hold the lingering and brooding expression of a
dreamer who saw far beyond the mortal ken of ordinary men.
The nose was finely shaped, sensitive and commanding in
strong contrast to the pale skin. When he spoke to me his
voice was clear and lucid. Words came from him, seriously
and slowly, yet full of power. I thought of the great
Emperor Ashoka. Then again I thought of Lord Buddha,
and I could not help feeling that in some distant way,
Nehru reminded me of them both, from all I had read of
the three of them in history and from what I beheld of Nehru
in person.

"What type of dancing do you like best of our four main
schools, Panditji?" I asked, searching his face.

"I love only the beauty of the movements. Watching you
tonight, I was more conscious of the dance than the actual
technique in which you executed your items. And that is the
test of great art—to conceal itself and give only the pure
vision of beauty to the spectator. Besides that, Ram Gopal,
I am unable to distinguish one style from another. How many
can? I cannot answer your query about the technique of the
various schools, but I can tell you that I liked your dance of
Shiva, Thillana and the Rajput serenade best of all the Indian
dancing I have seen."

I felt like saying, but did not, that I would be prepared to
dance all day and night for several days and nights, if it would
satisfy him.

How impressed I was by the beauty of his face. He was not

a young man, but he looked astonishingly youthful. He had long brooding eyes, like the Ajanta frescoes. And what a trim, slim silhouette his figure was. His actions were quick, his face active with a 'fire' and he answered readily any questions one asked him. There was the quality of culture and aristocracy in his face and gestures which only the high born could wear without seeming arrogant. He was so different from Gandhi. But then all vivid and great personalities are different from each other. Since the assassination of Gandhi, and the rebirth of India as a free nation, I have felt that the life of politicians must demand the greatest amount of tact, patience and strength that seem well nigh impossible for human nature to bear. Surely there must be some way in which all that 'body tension' can be relieved. How or in what manner, I do not know. Fishing and painting—like Churchill? Spinning cloth like Gandhi? Perhaps.

On the night of my introduction to Jawaharlal Nehru there was a dinner with many celebrities present. Sarojini Naidu sat quiet and impassive, which was rather unusual for her, since on previous occasions I had always known where she was at a reception or party by the large crowd that was in- evitably drawn to this woman. I asked someone why she looked so wan and quiet, and was told that she had recovered from one of her heart attacks that of late had become rather frequent.

I remember in 1944 travelling from Bombay to Poona with Sarojini and myself alone in the compartment. Here was a chance for her to relax and talk informally. It was at a time that anybody who spoke as he or she thought was either jailed or 'given notice'. She had just attended an Indian National Congress meeting in Bombay and was going to Poona for a rest. I thought to myself that, since she would be having the rest she badly needed in Poona, I might as well ask her what she thought about people, the situation at that time, and her views on music, literature and other subjects. She speaks with the most extraordinary flow of words it is possible to imagine.

I said: "Tell me, Sarojini, what personal views do you have on both Gandhi and Nehru? Not political views, but the personal slants you have on them—the little things you may have noticed about them in your very close and intimate touch with them."

There was no distant gazing out of the window, as some other Congresswomen affect when asked direct questions. Her answer came spontaneously from the heart, and I settled down to spend two of the most absorbing and interesting hours of my lifetime with her, as we sped through the gigantic western ghats.

"Gandhi is of course a very, very great soul. He is like a peasant in many ways. Simple to the point of absurdness sometimes, he sheds a light of greatness around him that even the most hardened are touched by. In many respects he is shrewd, cunning calculating, but that is natural, for he is a *banya* (tradesman)—and proud of it—by birth. But aside from all his greatness, there is a quality of sadness about him after the death of his two closest and dearest ones, his wife and his secretary. In his present state I have come closer to him, drawn perhaps by my maternal instincts as I would to a child—for Gandhi has the heart of a child in many ways, and all of its purity. He lives with God, and God surely dwells in his heart."

There was a pause. We sipped some tea. "And Nehru? What about him? How have you reacted to him 'offstage'? What about Nehru the man, as distinct from Nehru the dreamer and nation-builder? What difference have you noticed as compared to the Mahatma?" She smiled. Her smile comes as easily and naturally as that of a child. It is charming and bewitching with its gravity, sadness and yet has womanly and motherly warmth.

"We often argue, because Jawaharlal is very temperamental. We often debate furiously about something and then when things begin to get hot we break down and laugh!" She smiled again. "Humour is one advantage that those of us have who have had Western education, not the empty, superficial kind, but the true great, free education that one gets by study and travel in the West. I often pity the others working with us with their lack of humour and dry faces, and try to liven things up by bringing them to good humour.

"Now to return to Jawaharlal. He had many opportunities when young, in every way, that were denied Gandhi—his aristocratic birth, wealth, intensive education both abroad and in India, a revolutionary father, and his meeting with great intellects. His views are broader than those of Gandhi in many respects. He is a visionary who sees things as they are today, with a view to building them tomorrow and harmonising the world the day after." She paused. "It is of course hard to draw comparisons between them. Each is in a class by himself."

I thought to myself that Gandhi was like Krishna, the Divine One, whose eternal melody today, in the twentieth century, was one of peace and love, whose doctrine of non-violence the barbaric and machine-dominated West was incapable of understanding. Nehru reminded me of Arjuna, who fought bravely and vanquished the evil he saw about him through his great powers of mind and spirit. However, at times during that dinner I thought I detected, on occasional moments when his face was in repose, a rather pouting lower lip, and a certain weakness about his features and expression.

Jawaharlal ate only salads that night at dinner. I thought to myself that that was why he was able to have such a cool head and clear skin. There were quite a lot of prominent Congress members present—a very assorted variety, too, I noticed, when I looked closely. I saw a Congresswoman from the south, one who had gone to jail a few times, 'enjoyed' its heat, suffered the usual fevers, and had come out a much publicised 'national heroine'. I had a sly conviction that she spent more time in jail building herself up through a well directed publicity campaign into a 'cultured pearl' variety of heroine, than the genuine article. Where before the finest silks were the order of the day for her and those of her superficial type, she was now walking in sheep's clothing, swathed in shawls of homespun *Kahddar*, which she wore with obvious discomfort. In the first flush of our growing spirit of independence, I noticed that India was not without her spiritual quislings who would do anything to remain in the limelight. There were some millionaires' daughters there, too, that evening with the most magnificent diamonds dragging down their ears, and necklaces to match. They wore the usual veils too, slightly finer than *Khaddar*, which they told me was 'homespun', but which looked 'millspun' to me, and was worn, I was sure, more for reasons of advertisement than simplicity.

I accepted an invitation to tour for the convalescent British and Indian troops in hospitals scattered throughout the length and breadth of India. Had I only known what this meant! In peace-time itself, travelling was by no means easy, but to try and do the same thing with a troupe in war-time was to court disaster. Come what may, I felt that I had to do something, and dancing for convalescent human beings was one of the best contributions I could make during such times. We zigzagged all over India, only to find that when some representative of a chosen area did not turn up, it was because he was not told in time, with the result that there was no adequate room for us to live in except parking on the station platforms or waiting-rooms. And all our human needs had to be carried out under the most embarrassing situations. Whenever we started dancing the South Indian Tanjore suite of dances, the troops from the Punjab would start shouting for the songs to be sung in Punjabi, and the opposite happened when we were touring in Hyderabad and North Indian singing accompanied the regional Kathak dances of the north.

Aside from the terrible discomforts, the food was uneatable. Vegetables were scarce, the milk was watered, if not given to us in powdered form in tins—with instructions that sounded better than the milk tasted. And the complete disorganisation of this first ENSA tour, which was sincerely put into action, was under the general direction of my friend, Eric Dunstan, who would have needed an army to run the whole show efficiently. I remember how happy and free I felt when I finished my last performance.

As soon as I had returned to Bangalore after dancing in Bombay, I was filled with depression and frustration.

"Why don't you carry on with your school?" my mother suggested wisely. She knew that I was feeling unhappy and full of nervous tensions that only dancing could sublimate.

"Yes, Mother, I think it's a good idea. I can run my school, and when I tour India, some of the teachers that I shall bring from Tanjore and Malabar in the south can carry on my work." And that was precisely what I did from 1940 onwards. I engaged the services of several dancers, Ellappa Mudaliar and Gowrie Ammal among them, who worked closely with Bala Saraswati, greatest living woman dancer of 'Dasi Attam' and Muthukumaran Pillai from Mayavaram in the Tanjore district. He worked on very much the same lines as Meenakshisundaram Pillai. Also Kunju Nair and Kunchunni, two students of the Kerala school of the Poet Vallathol in Shoranur, and a Kathak dance master who was mostly drugged with opium and slept continuously in a world of dreams. His term of employment lasted a very short time and I was glad to see him go, for his habit of 'seeing things' were infecting some of my other musicians, and I was frightened that some of the dancers might try this deadly drug.

But for me the greatest good luck came when that long cherished dream of getting Kunchu Kurup—about whom I have already written—to come and teach me exclusively came true. We worked for as much as eight to ten hours a day over a period of five years. I also went to Meenakshis-undaram Pillai, the greatest teacher of 'Dasi Attam', who was also fully versed in the principles of Bharata Natya Sastra and the dramatic Bhagavata Mela Nataka of Soolamangalam (a village in the district of Tanjore). Meenakshisundaram Pillai's ancestors had derived much from its style and technique, and this great dance master himself could dance beautifully portions from it. The first time I went to Tanjore, I was taken by my good friend, the eminent Art critic of classical Indian dancing and music, E. Krishna Iyer. How indebted I am to him for all the time, patience and trouble he took in revealing so much to me that otherwise would have been difficult to understand of the rich heritage that South India has of its Tamil drama, dance and music.

On the right-hand corner of the large garden that was my home, with Father's permission, I had constructed a garden studio. The stage was covered with a tiled roof. The floor was slightly raised. The 'auditorium' was large enough to accommodate about a hundred people. And it was in that studio that all my pupils came and worked from morning till night.

Mrinalini Sarabahai was one of my first students. She had never learnt the full programme of 'Dasi Attam' before. But at my school she studied the technique and made rapid progress under the expert guidance of Muthukumaran Pillai.

She also studied Kathak dancing. I remember how lithe and graceful her body was and how delicately she danced. When I danced in Bangalore and later in Madras and Calcutta during the war, it was Mrinalini whom I took as my partner. It was during her stay in Bangalore that she met and later married her husband. Every morning, Mrinalini, who lived at the other end of Bangalore, would be given a lift in the car of two sisters, also students of my school. Both these sisters came of a distinguished family from Coorg in Mysore State. The elder, Nina Thimayya, looked like some golden bronze, or ivory Goddess in beauty of face and form. Boli Cariappa, the younger sister, was just like a young Garbo—but a brunette Garbo, with dark, long eyes and the most beautiful lips and smile. These two sisters, living miles away from my garden studio, were good enough to bring Mrinalini in their car from her rooms to my studio every single day for a period of years. And how they worked!

Neither Mrinalini nor Nina Thimayya had the vaguest idea about the Tanjore or Kathakali dances, stage costuming, lighting or the craft of the theatre. But they did all they could to learn. Boli, Nina's sister, studied Kathak dancing because she said that that was the style she liked. But after some months this beautiful girl tired of it, found it difficult and strenuous, and gave up. Nina, the elder sister, worked harder than ever and discovered that in the Tanjore dance her soul found its highest expression. She worked harder than Mrinalini and other students at the centre. And what glorious eyes she had—large, deep brown, with curving lids, fine nose and small mouth. Her ivory fair complexion grew golden under the strenuous rehearsals from which I demanded everything that was best from each of my pupils studying technique under my instructors and the finishing touches of the dance from me.

However much one demanded of Nina, she never flinched.

I have seldom seen any girl work as hard, consistently or as long as she did in those days of 1940. Sometimes Mrinalini would dance side by side with Nina. Nina, fair and exquisite, Mrinalini, dark and lissom with rather large feet and hands compared to the finer beauty of her fairer partner. But when they did the invocational dance, the 'Alarippu' together, and the rhythmic sequence called the 'Jathisvaram', they looked like two Ajanta frescoes moving in perfect harmony and rhythm. Mrinalini moved her body with greater pliability than Nina, but Nina's beauty of face and arms outshone that of Mrinalini.

Muthukumaran Pillai, a superb actor and dancer in 'Dasi Attam' himself, would insist that expression was vital to bring life to the various *Padams* or devotional love songs. Gowrie Ammal from Mylapore, Madras (in her time one of the great temple dancers of 'Dasi Attam') had come to teach expression and gestures at my school. For hours she would repeat a series of *mudras* and accompany these gestures with the most delicate and exquisite facial expressions, called *abhinaya*. Nina would follow closely, absolutely absorbed in the story being enacted before her by this great actress. 'Krishna Ne Baganae' was a love story of simple beauty in which the God Krishna was invited to come to the devotee and abide within her being. Mrinalini, learning this *padam*, could not, hard as she tried, get the exact expression on her face for this passage of dance. Her gestures, poses and rhythm were good but she could not at that time infuse life into the expressions of her face. . . . So I made her practise the nine *rasas* of the Kathakali dance to get the muscles of her face to move with delicate nuance and expression. I think it helped her a great deal.

The classes began at eight in the morning and went on until sunset, with a break for lunch. The girls would come to my sitting-room-cum-library, filled with antiques and

Rajput miniatures, and rest and read. After lunch we would discuss the next day's work. And it was during those respites that I used to talk to them and tell them about the art of making up their eyes, their hair styles and the costumes they should wear, depending also on the story or character they were portraying.

"Remember this," I would say sternly to them, "unless your dances are brought to life by a study of the 'Bhagavad Gita', the 'Upanishads', and the simply written works of the great teachers of philosophy, both past and present, your performance will be dull, lifeless, dead. You must know why and what you do in each dance, which is impossible unless you 'feel' it. And you can only feel these legendary stories and infuse them with life if you study the old texts."

I remember one recital we gave at the Town Hall in Bangalore. It was for some war-time charity and I arranged the choreography. Nina would stand on my right, Mrinalini on my left, with myself in the centre. We all wore white and specially designed costumes. It was the first time the public in Bangalore saw the ancient Tanjore dance style done with my choreographic patterning and danced by both sexes. The 'Dasi Attam' is usually danced by women alone but today many young men dance it in Madras and other parts of India. "If women use the Kathakali technique and dance styles and perform in public, should we not do the same with the 'Dasi Attam' and perform those portions of it best suited to us?" is the invariable reply one gets today from male students.

The 'Dasi Attam' of Tanjore derives from the Bhagavata Mela Natska, the male dance drama *par excellence* of the village of Soolamangalam in Tanjore district itself. So there are portions of this dance which both the male and female students of Hindu Natya can perform. The Bhagavata Mela Nataka dance drama is of course far, far older than the 'Dasi Attam, which one sees performed all over Southern India. In this respect it must have the antiquity and tradition of Kathakali Temple dancing performed again exclusively and only by men in Malabar. There is a picturesque dance drama in which a number of women perform in the great temple of Siva in Tanjore itself. It is called a *Kuravanji* which means a dance drama enacted by women. Of course the whole drama is conducted by a *Nattuvanar*, or Dance Master.

My guru, Meenakshisundaram Pillai, had often conducted many such *Kuravanji* dramas. He used to tell me that his greatest female pupil of those times, a *Devadasi*, 'Servant of God' called Jeevaratnam, the Daughter of Kalyani Ammal from Kumbakonam, used to dance the title role of Valli (the heroine of the *Kuravanji*) with such grace and perfection that he was reduced to tears. "I used to stop singing. The *talas* (steel cymbals) in my hands would drop into my lap as I sat cross-legged conducting the music. I used to get carried away by the beauty of her acting. I cannot imagine ever again seeing such perfection of expression. And when she danced the purely rhythmic sequences, all the other girls I had trained seemed like wooden dolls by comparison. Once in every Master's life comes that perfection, that divinity incarnate, and Jeevaratnam was that girl whom I had the great joy of training from the time she first learnt to walk." He was always deeply moved when talking of this wonderful dancer. I had seen her perform in Mysore several years before her death. And it was the dancing of this girl that had inspired Rukmini Devi of Adyar to learn all she could from my guru and Master, Meenakshisundaram Pillai. It was one of the greatest tragedies to the world of Indian dancing that Jeevaratnam died of smallpox in the early thirties.

During a visit to Kumbakonam I visited the house of her mother, Kalyani Ammal, who I had been told had a great love affair with my guru, Meenakshisundaram, when they were both young. Jeevaratnam, it was rumoured, was the 'flower' of their passion. Perhaps that accounted for the tender care and love he bestowed on her, also for the tears that he shed when he talked of this great dancer. When I visited the house of the old lady, Kalyani Ammal, she lovingly took out the *talai saman*, a jewel traditional with Devadasis, worn on their slicked black heads. She showed me the *manga malai*, a temple jewel of rare antiquity, encrusted with rubies, diamonds and emeralds, which Jeevaratnam had worn, and most precious of all, her anklet bells which brought such music to the Tala, or timing, of her matchless footwork. They were now like relics. How moved we all were as the old mother explained everything with tender affection and details to us. I say 'we', for there were the usual crowd of relations that could not understand why Ram Gopal should want to see these relics.

It was in Kumbakonam that Varalakshi and Bhanumati, another exciting pair of dancers, had lived and worked with their great Master, Vadivelu Pillai. Jeevaratnam, Varalakshi and my great master and guru, Meenakshisundaram Pillai are all dead now, perhaps somewhere above in a temple worthy of the gods themselves my guru conducts the heavenly dance performances of these dancers whom the few mortals that remember their dance on this earth cherish for ever.

My school overflowed with pupils. Some came for the novelty, others for the chance to learn a little, and still others to look upon the art of dancing in the same spirit in which I had dedicated my life. It took me many years to find out that the ideals I worked for were not exactly those that many of the so-called students shared. Very few of them paid me anything, although Nina Thimayya was one of the few who did, and regularly too. I could never resist a 'hard luck' story. It was the usual theme with a lot of the other students, both male or female. Their story became a theme song of "No papa, no mama . . . very poor . . . you teach me everything . . . I do what you like afterwards". But the more serious pupils who joined my school were those who gave my masters and myself great satisfaction. They made up for the ungrateful students.

There was Krishna Rao and his wife, Chandrabagha Devi. Krishna had been my boyhood friend and enthused by my insatiable quest for learning all I could, and by my dancing, he also studied with the great gurus I had worked under, and he and his beautiful wife gave many outstanding performances. How magnificent they both looked, dancing like Shakti and Shakta, the male-female principle of Indian mythology. They have since opened a school where Krishna Rao (who is also a brilliant professor in science at the local college) with the help of Chandrabaga, imparts the knowledge of dancing to students from Mysore State and Bangalore itself.

There was the very interesting case of a Parsi girl. She was a student of Viennese dancing which she was studying in Bombay, and, being interested in some complicated system of philosophy, wanted to study at my school, because she felt that through dancing she would uncover her past incarnations. The reasons she gave for asking to be a pupil of my school were all very complicated. But, moved by pity, I consented to her studying there and she made fair progress in acquiring the style and technique. But, somehow, she could never immerse herself in the spirit of Hinduism, and try as she could, there was an alien spirit that pervaded her Indian dancing. I was impressed by her work and perseverance, though. I have often wondered what became of her and whether she kept to her Indian dancing or was seeking some other outlet for discovering her previous incarnations.

There were other students, Shevanti from Bombay, whose every line and movement were filled with grace and beauty; Janaki, a young Brahmin girl from Madras, who moved like Parvati, Goddess of the Dance herself; Tara, the dancer from the Punjab, who had grace and vitality; Rajeshwar, whose slim waist was the envy of every girl in the company and who danced like a gazelle. These pupils are only a few of exceptional talent who worked in my garden studio. There are others, too numerous to mention, who could not stay the course and found it difficult to continue.

Crowning all those years of work and study, was an invitation to appear at the All India Dance Festival in Bombay in 1944. There, with the foremost dancers gathered together from the four corners of India, the leading critic of Bombay, D. C. Shah wrote:

"Ram Gopal stood head and shoulders above the rest. Ram Gopal's was the smallest troupe at the festival and yet his two performances are amongst the season's greatest highlights."

In addition to this, the leading critics who organised the festival had organised a poll, and my dancing topped the list by a vast majority of votes. It was not that such praise flattered me. On the contrary, it made me realise that such adulation as the public gave my efforts should spur me on to greater heights. I would work harder and give more, and more, of the best within me. If I could convey something of the Truth of God through my dancing, and if I had to sacrifice and suffer and relinquish everything for fulfilling that ideal, then I would do so. For whatever moments of 'Truth' were revealed to the audience in my dances made any sacrifices worth while.

I was also invited to organise and dance in the All India Dance Festival held at Delhi. I had always loved dancing in Delhi. The north held a fascination and beauty for me that was hard to define. A self-effacing and kindly lady, Nirmala Joshi, was one of the organisers of that festival. Also invited to appear was a Kathakali troupe from Malabar. And it was here that I renewed acquaintance with my friend, the great actor-dancer Ravunni Menon.

An amusing incident occurred at this festival. During one of the evening shows of Kathakali with its traditional make-up, costuming and performance, the North Indian public started to shout and stamp their feet. "We do not want to see this mask dancing and face making. We want something else. . . ." And so they shouted in the various dialects of the north. The stamping and shouting became a roar . . . the curtain came down . . . and it was explained to the Kathakali dancers that the reason was as follows: "Your dancing is so powerful and dynamic and frightening that the public were moved to shout . . . and that curtain? Oh well, er . . . that silly stage manager, he has made a mistake!" I do not know how convinced these simple dancers were. I do know and I did see, however, that the all-seeing, and flashing eyes of the portly Ravunni Menon (noted for his exceptionally powerful and virile dancing) twinkled with diabolical laughter and rage at the same time. Surely this was another *rasa* or sentiment, I thought, that I had never seen this great actor assume before in the Kerala Kalamandalam, where I had first watched his dance classes.

This is the sequel. Two evenings later this same Katha-kali troupe, headed by Ravunni Menon, were scheduled to appear for the first performance. As their make-up is a long and complicated process, requiring several hours, Ravunni Menon and his troupe had come much earlier and, lying on their mats, subjected themselves to the skill of the expert Kathakali make-up artist. At about six o'clock on that particular evening, Nirmala Joshi came running to my hotel.

"There has been a slight change, Ram Gopal. Would you dance this evening for the first performance? You see, the Vicerine and her party are coming, and lots of V.I.P's and

(*photo: Jas. D. O'Callaghan*)

"The Temptation of Lord Buddha"

As a Rajput Prince in a Kathak dance pose

after what happened to the Kathakali dancing a few days ago, the committee of the festival have decided to replace them with a performance of your troupe instead. Would you dance, do you mind?" Nirmala asked rather nervously.

I could not refuse. If that was the decision of the Committee, then I would do as they wished. Then it occurred to me that that very afternoon I had seen Ravunni Menon with so much reverence and humility enter the dressing-rooms and prepare himself for that evening's performance. "Nirmala, what is going to happen to the Kathakali dancers? Ravunni Menon is a great dancer in his own field. What will he think? Have you told him? He is under the impression, as we all are, that his is to be the first performance. I don't want him to think or feel that I have taken his performance away from him because of the distinguished audiences that are going to be present this evening. Look, you get someone to explain to him everything tactfully. It will be a tough job but for God's sake don't let him get annoyed. I couldn't bear to hurt his feelings. Please, please be as tactful as possible."

Nirmala hurried away, promising to do all she could. I was, frankly, worried, and anxious. I would not like that sort of treatment meted out to me. I was annoyed at this sudden change of plans. But what could I do?

This is what happened later. Nirmala had found somebody else to tell Ravunni Menon of the change. By this time, an hour before the performance was due to commence, Ravunni Menon was majestically arrayed in his full regalia of head-dress, billowing skirts, red jacket, jewels and his splendid make-up. He had, as I knew from my study in Malabar, already become the character he was going to dance. When it finally dawned on him, through the tactful interpreter, that his performance was cancelled, Ravunni Menon, whose gentle disposition belied a very violent temperament when aroused, now unleashed his disappointment. I was in the

L

adjoining rooms allocated for each troupe of artists. I thought a hurricane had hit the theatre. Peering through my doorway, I could see that Ravunni Menon was giving one of the most inspired of his performances, but it was off stage. He scorched and reduced to ashes everyone and everything in that dressing-room. Eyes blazing, voice bellowing, he asked why such an insult was directed against him, he demanded that he go on the stage and violently threatened anybody who would dare stop him from performing that evening. He did not care who was or was not coming, he would dance.

"Now get out, all of you, you blithering sons of donkeys, you sons of weak-willed goats." Ravunni Menon roared at them in Malayalam.

Seeing this impressive Kathakali master burst into such a torrent of anger and disappointment made me full of sympathy and pity for what had taken place. I decided to walk straight into the lion's den. . . . I would try and pacify him. "They are a lot of mud-heads, fools, to have humiliated you. They should have told you about this change of programme this morning . . . but to tell you shortly before you are to go on . . . why, it is cruel, unforgivable," I went on. I soothed him. I spoke to him. But he was like a child. Tears streamed from his face. He walked up and down all the time and bellowed the most dire consequences if he was not permitted to dance.

"You know what, Ravunni? They have had the boldness to ask me to dance . . . and at only such short notice . . . as if I could go on now. . . . After seeing you and the pain it has caused you . . ." I added.

"You are going to dance instead of me? Did you ask them to remove me? . . . You didn't. So they have tried to brush me aside lightly? All right, let them try lifting that curtain this evening. Let them try getting those lights to shine!" Ravunni Menon looked as though he was holding some invisible trump card and I wondered what he was going to do.

Later I was told that some high dignitary, some landowner from the province where Ravunni came from, soothed and spoke to him. And it seemed that, having respect for the venerable landowner who spoke to him, Ravunni's anger abated. The signal was clear. Nirmala, in the meantime, eyes twinkling with excitement at the storm that had seemed to have passed, came to me and said: "It's all right now . . . I think we've managed it. He'll be calm now. Are you ready, Ram?"

Nina Thimayya who was with me and Janaki, both went on that evening. The first item went all right; it was a musical interlude in praise of Ganapati, the elephant-headed god who removed all obstacles. This was the introductory musical interlude. Then the two girls, Nina Thimayya and Janaki, danced. Following the first item, the Alarippu, Janaki went on to perform her solo dance, the Jathisvaram (a purely rhythmic dance) to the Raga or melody of Chakravagam. Half-way through her dance, which Janaki was performing very well, she came to the portion where she takes a running leap to the right side and then repeats this to the left before finishing up in a very fast rhythmic pattern of the feet accompanied by her arms and hands. As she leapt into the air, something had happened, for instead of landing on her feet, she landed flat on her back and one of her bangles ripped into her arms, cutting it badly. Try as she could after this, she could not, did not seem able to move, some strange power seemed to will her not to dance. Tears streaming from her face, she rushed to Nina Thimayya, and to her dressing-room.

I dismissed it as just an accident. These things happen to the best of dancers. It was my turn next. The music started, the drums were beating their swift tempo; I prepared to go

swiftly out on to the stage. I said my prayers. As I danced
out on to the stage and was tracing the quick pattern of my
entrance on the boards, the lights flickered, dimmed, went
out. There was a gasp from the audience. The next moment
I was dancing in the dark.

Retracing my steps I walked to the wings. The music
came. In a few moments the electrician had repaired the fuse
and the lights were on again. Again my cue, the music began
. . . again I was dancing as if nothing had happened. At precisely the same moment as before the lights fused again. The
audience, with the Vicerine and other V.I.P.s started to get
restless, somebody laughed and the tension broke. That saved
the situation—for the audience.

Once more I was in the wings, this time praying harder
than ever, and I realised that Ravunni Menon's anger was not
without meaning. I remembered his veiled threats of "Let
them try getting those lights to shine". So, using all of my
own will power, I pitted my forces against his, and using
every ounce of concentration, danced again for the third
time on to that stage. And come what may, lights or no
lights, I would dance. Nothing happened except that the
lights flickered again tremulously a few times; but for that
item and the remainder of the programme, all went well.
Everybody was pleased. Of course, I had heard of the
'Thought Magic' that could be used for all manner of ends.
As I walked to my dressing-room, I looked for Ravunni
Menon. I was told that in the early part of the programme
he had left, storming. That night, Nina Thimayya and I lit
an extra incense stick and oil light to Ganesa, God of
Obstacles, for having protected us from further catastrophe.

Kathakali dancing is seen at its best when performed in its
natural setting at night with blazing oil torches and lights,
and on a temple or village lawn. The same dancers performing those same dynamic dances on the stage of an electrically

lit theatre lose a great deal of their magic and mystery. It would take an expert of the theatre to illuminate and present these dancers and bring out what only the natural setting of the Indian night and those oil torches can create. Also the vast public of Northern India are removed from the styles, customs and dances of Southern India. Many of my friends, from men of letters to university students, complain that the music and singing of the south irritate and bore them. It made me realise how complex, contradictory and strange the continent of India was to Indians themselves. Often, I myself, coming upon some new ceremony or ritual during one of my tours in India, would be amazed to find something that made me feel 'strange' and foreign to the spectacle before me.

India is so vast. In South India alone the peoples of Mysore, where I was born, would find it hard to understand the Tamil-speaking peoples of Madras a few hundred miles away, and the peoples of Andhra could not speak anything but their own dialect of Telugu, and when these three peoples of the south would meet at some function or festival day, they all conversed in English! I wonder now what language we will all have to speak in India? The original Sanskrit, from which all the varying dialects of India are derived, would be the only solution, for we Indians love clinging to our 'mother tongue' of the local province where we were born, and are loth to cast it aside for anything less than the universal language of India's ancient sages and philosophers—Sanskrit.

When a leading magazine from Bombay asked for a series of articles on classical dancing and the work in my school, it was Serozh Dadachanji, the art and film critic, who was assigned the job. Dadachanji and myself had been friends since the early years of the war, having met in Bombay. His encyclopædic knowledge of films, stories, stars and everything connected with films was something that amazed me. He wrote the critiques for all the American and European films that appeared in Bombay. I have never read any reviews comparable to those by this immensely talented writer. Later Dadachanji and I co-authored a book on Indian dancing which has enjoyed a considerable success. He was the friend who rushed to my side, from Bombay to Bangalore, when I lost my beloved mother.

During my stay in Bangalore I was at a display of the virile 'Kathak' male folk dancers of the far north to which I was taken by my friend Major-General Akbar Khan, who was good enough to organise this spectacular dance performance one night in late summer. It was there that I was introduced to Michael Rouse, who was in the British Army. His work covered not only India, but later Burma and Java. He was very popular in his regiment because of his understanding and knowledge of Indians. Consequently, when the war was over, and before his return to England, I asked him whether he would like to accept the work of being my company organiser and manager. Of all the people who have handled companies of Hindu dancers and musicians, Michael Rouse was easily the most tactful, alert and most beloved. When I returned to England in 1947, after the war, Mrs. Rouse, Michael's mother, invited me to come and holiday with them in Newquay. Much as I admire the great beauty of all the English countryside in spring and summer, it is Cornwall with its air of brooding mystery and beauty that will always hold a special place in my heart.

I remember the lakes, woods and rocky beaches I visited on my first trip there. Michael pointed to one of the lakes and said: "That is the lake from which the sword Excalibur was given to King Arthur and later vanished into it." My mind went back to the teacher at school in Bangalore, and I remembered her stories of King Arthur and his Knights of the Round Table. Cornwall is filled with stones, and rocks and trees and castles, all impregnated with legend and myths.

And most Cornishmen always referred to their land as 'Our Country'. One day I said: "What do you mean, our country? Isn't it all part of England?"

"Oh no, Ram . . ." came the indignant reply from Michael, "you see, the English are foreigners here. We have lived here from . . . well, as far as memory goes back."

It was only after travelling very extensively during my three dance tours in England that I found the term 'our country' could mean not England itself as a whole, but some bit of Wales, Devon or Cornwall!

I remember how scared I was when I saw my first hedge-hog, and because of its stillness, and slowness, imagined it was going to attack me. Michael and his mother laughed at me.

"You needn't laugh, Michael," I said, "do you remember the story you told me of the time you were attacked by a snake in the Burma jungle. You were very embarrassed, Michael, by what happened then. You were marching your Indian battalion through a forest path; you, representing the British Raj, were leading them, and then, when you came to that wretched little snake, you stood back rather grandly and asked one of your Indian soldiers to kill it. Instead, the whole lot of them stood there and smiled at you. In order to save the prestige of the British you were forced to snatch a stick from someone's hand and then you killed the poor thing. The men knew it was a harmless grass snake and one of the almost blind species! But you did feel very brave at having dis-patched that little reptile, didn't you, but not without being frightened. So I cannot understand why you laugh at me and this funny little hedgehog," I explained, trying to cover my embarrassment from Mrs. Rouse, who was very amused by the story of her son's bravery in the Burmese jungle.

"I am rather shaken, Michael," she said, with a twinkle in her blue eyes. "I thought, from all those letters you wrote me that my handsome young son was fighting the war single-handed, and I now learn that you were killing snakes instead!" We three had a very good laugh. Cornwall was my first initiation into the sacred soil that is part of England and her great traditions.

CHAPTER TWELVE

Gods, Sages and Yogis

SHORTLY after returning to India from Europe, to that beautiful big, rambling colonial house with its exotic garden, my mother grew listless. There was a war on, the doctors said, and one could not get the necessary drugs. The diagnosis they gave her proved to be quite inadequate. They said she had anæmia, when in fact she was suffering from a virulent consumption. From a strong, healthy and vital woman, I began to notice how this deadly disease gradually, slowly sapped her vitality, and under one's very eyes her whole frame faded like a waning moon. Pale, ivory and ghostly her pallor became. It was painful to see my father bend over her bed. He was in his eighties. With feeble whisperings they would both converse. Again I had to prove all the scriptural works I had read by trying to draw comfort from them . . . by telling myself that the end of everything we call Life was but a new beginning. But why all this pain? Why should two exemplary and beloved parents have to suffer this? I found many answers within me, some satisfying, others disturbing. One night, my elder sister called me. There was that tone in her voice which made me feel 'intuitively' that Mother's sufferings would soon be over.

Running to the bedside of my mother, my family and I gathered beside her. In her tender and slanting Mongolian eyes there was peace. She said a few words to all of us, too sacred for writing . . . and there, in full view of us, she gave one little deep sigh as if she was very tired, and her head turned to the left on her white pillow . . . she was gone. . . . And very shortly after that, Father passed over, too. They had been so close together, it did not seem right that one should live while the other had gone on.

I did not cry with any particular anguish. I did not feel my heart break. I felt numb. Perhaps that great consciousness of philosophy and Occult truth that I had so avidly studied had something to do with it, perhaps something within me died inside. It was during the period that followed their passing over that my interest in a search for truth with the 'Wise' ones continued. I read all I could—re-read the old books that had been my favourites, the 'Bhagavad Gita', the 'Upanishads', the Teachings of Lord Buddha. I derived some comfort. But when I was not working at my dancing, or when I was not busy appearing on the stage itself, I visited and sought every 'Holy Man' whom I knew of or could become acquainted with. And in this strange restless quest, I found so much that I admired and much that I despised. I had seen something of a certain Indian Theosophist during this period. But I found that his leanings towards religion were purely for extracting money from susceptible victims. And those strange, incensed, half-lit rooms of 'initiation' were nothing but an excuse for perverted indulgences. That sort of hypocrisy was not for me. I had more sympathy for the flesh peddlers of the streets compared to this black monster's evil.

India has such a rich and varied assortment of truth embodied in its great men and sages. And the opposite is true, too. For at many of the *ashrams* I had visited in India where the 'genuine' Sages resided I had found that the place was usually filled with *chelas* (disciples) and *Swamis* (holy men), and lots of hysterical society men and women, not to mention the millionaires of both the 'touchable' and 'untouchable' castes. Touchable or untouchable, those millionaires who visit these Holy Sages to glean peace within themselves (or perhaps, as some of the deluded ones come, to ask how their stocks are going to soar in the coming seasons) are all alike 'stilled' by the peace emanating from the Great Ones to whom they come to pay homage. And it is here that I could plainly see that the vast majority of people milling around the central figure of the particular sage, all had the timid and cowardly expressions of 'escapists'. They were all running away from life. They were taking the easy way out by sitting at the feet of these Holy Ones. Such a negative attitude helped them to postpone merely what the true seeker of realisation faced boldly and fearlessly in the face.

I had a psychic experience shortly after my mother died. I was asleep one night in my bedroom and the door leading into my sitting-room-library, which was decorated and furnished in Rajputana style, was open. Standing in one corner of the room was the matchless bronze image of Gauri, the Mother aspect of Divinity, and there were some lights burning around her. A pink shaded electric light was always kept alight in the sitting-room and the glow of its shade with that of the lights around Gauri, shed a soft pale light into my room. And one could see quite clearly the outline of every-thing in the room.

I was sleeping very soundly when I had the sensation of a heavy hand placed between my throat and chest. I half opened my eyes, and suddenly was gripped with a great fear. For, vaguely outlined beside me was a great shape, sitting cross-legged, dressed in white. I remember gathering my will power and controlling the terrible fear that arose within me, and very, very gradually I opened my eyes, looking out from under my lids. And there beside me was a *Yogi*, long, flowing white hair, sacred thread around his chest, sitting cross-legged, his right hand extended and placed on my chest.

For a moment I panicked . . . my throat grew parched . . . what was he trying to do? I felt a comforting vibration coming through the touch of his hand on me. But, being the first experience of its kind I had ever had, I was very afraid. Nothing like that had happened to me in my sleep before. I started to pray with all of my heart, and gradually the figure began to levitate at my side, rising into the air, seated in exactly the posture described, legs folded and body held erect. Right before my eyes, it floated a few feet off the green carpet and out through the doorway and then disappeared from view.

This was not an hallucination. I had not read any books about *Yoga* or ghosts or anything that could have fired my imagination . . . and then within me I felt a voice whisper: "All the time the angels see and the eye of God watches . . . and when his children are troubled and confused and seek his help, he directs and sends his chosen angels to come in various ways and moments. Do not assail your heart with fear."

I felt calm after that. When I switched on the light at my bedside and looked at the time it was two o'clock. Saying my prayers over and over again, I fell asleep. The next morning, when I awoke, I had peace within me. I related my experience to my sister, Flo.

"But you've always heard me tell you of the experiences I have had. And your brother, too. And you know that neither of us has very much belief in the supernatural. Don't you remember how Jumbo (my brother's nickname because of his strength and prowess in boxing) was flung off his bed, the shoes under his bed sent flying into the air! And the other experience I had of the door of my room being twisted and turned as if someone were trying to get in? Nobody could have come in. The door was unlocked and I was sleeping in a room occupied by the two of us—elder sister and myself. And yet this persistent twisting of the door-handle went on all night. In the morning we two girls asked each other whether we had both heard the same thing? And how scared I was to find that this very same noise had been heard all that night by our sister. There are spirits in this house . . . there always have been."

I remembered all the stories I had heard from her and my brother, and Gulab, my father's Rajput valet. Gulab even said: "*Sono Baba*" (my childhood name), "there is an old temple site under the fern-house and a big hamadryad cobra is living there. You can see many lights sometimes on full moon nights. Sometimes it comes, sometimes, it doesn't." It was a phenomenon that seemed inexplicable to me, because neither my father nor my mother had ever mentioned anything to me about this.

A few weeks after Mother's death, Nina Thimayya and I drove down to a little village situated at the back of Nandi Hills, those blue-gum tree studded hills where I had first met Gandhi. We drove on to the most inaccessible and primitive road, and stopped at some distance from a renowned *Yogi*, called Hanumantha Swamiji. We walked a short distance to a tiled roof and mud-walled building consisting of a few rooms. And coming out to greet us was one of the sprightliest and most loving of *Yogis* I have ever met.

"I am glad you have come. Why did you not come earlier?" he said, eyes lighting up as though he had known me a very long time. With this very simple but exceedingly powerful *Yogi*, I had some of the most interesting experiences I have ever known. I met him often. On one occasion a temple was being built, and they needed four great rock-hewn Juggernaut wheels. These great, giant-sized stone wheels carry a miniature temple, priest and Deity on certain festive occasions. "Will you dance here in the village Town Hall? And could the money be utilised for both the school of village children and the wheels of the chariot?" he asked me one afternoon, during a visit.

"I'll gladly do so, Swamiji," I answered.

And some weeks later, partnered by Nina Thimayya and some of my musicians, I danced at the local Town Hall. How pleased he was with the performance! His blessings more than compensated for whatever we had hoped to raise.

One day, some months later, he asked me to come for a 'blessing and grace' that he desired to give to me, alone. That afternoon, led by him, we set out for the hills that surrounded his village hermitage. We walked for about an hour, and after climbing up some of the very steep and rocky hills, arrived at last at the mouth of some recesses that looked more like shelters than caves. Here, I thought, we would both sit down and meditate. Instead, he beckoned to me, saying: "Follow me, we have almost arrived at the temple." What temple? I failed to understand. As I followed him, watching my step carefully as it was growing dark, I suddenly found myself alone. My friend had vanished! I looked around, called out, and for a few moments there was only the echoing silence. Peering at me from a crevice in the rock he said: "You'll have to squeeze in. Don't worry we have lights inside." And in the smallest circle of the rock, with barely enough room to enter sideways, I slowly slid through.

Inside, all was dark. My eyes could not as yet get accustomed to the blackness, even though night was falling outside. But what a stillness, what peace there was within! It was indescribable. Once my eyes had grown accustomed to the cave temple within these enormous rocks, I could discern the lights and the place of *puja* with its freshly-plucked flowers and the incense. And it was during the meditation which followed that I was initiated into the realms of Truth and things of the Spirit.

"How did you discover this hidden temple?" I eagerly enquired as we were walking back with a hurricane lamp which he held in his hands.

"It's a very long story . . . my master led me there . . . but only the elect are taken there. You have a great work to perform and you need great strength for it. That is why I wanted you to come this evening."

He was a simple postmaster fulfilling a very ordinary job, living with a family. And then the 'call' came, as it does to so many in various ways. He had devoted his entire life to uplifting the illiterate village folk by tending them with herbal cures, prayers and the like. Over a period of years a special train was run, filled with pilgrims, for his blessings and his cures, both physical and spiritual. On those days the hermitage was peopled with thousands of devotees who came not only from the surrounding villages and Bangalore itself, but also from other parts of India.

In spite of all the riches and enormous temples that people offered to give him and build there for him, he had chosen the most ascetic life of service and lived, if anything, even more frugally on herbs and vegetables and milk from his own acre of land. He led his cows into the hills himself, and it was said that he fell into mystic trances while his flock grazed. He was always dressed in handspun that he tied around his lithe youthful figure, and a shirt made of the same material. His face was stern, unsmiling. Only the eyes were kindly and shone with an uncanny power lit from within. He died a few years ago, and in one of his last communications to me he said that whatever happened to him in the 'flesh' his spirit would be with me. I derived much comfort and strength from this great *Yogi* of the hills.

"Arise! Awake! Seek out the great ones and get understanding," says the ancient teaching of the Upanishads. The Upanishad begins by laying down the doctrine of action without attachment resulting in *Paramatman*, light of all lights, which are both aspects of the same Sun. Pious Hindus immersing themselves at dawn into the waters of the sacred rivers cry out: "He who is there, that being there, He is myself." Identity of the Light within the soul is ONE with the Light of the Sun.

Seek out the great ones and get understanding! Always this is what I try to do. I first saw a photograph of Ramana Maharishi when I was still at school. I thought to myself: 'He looks exactly like my father, only his eyes have more kindliness, and unlike Father's, they are not stern.'

Friends of mine with whom I was driving from Bangalore to Madras, by car, decided to stay the night at a rest house. "Look, we are not far from Arunachala, the Hill of the Holy beacon. Let's drive there and watch the blaze of light that will be lit on this holy hill and then get the *darshan* (blessing) of Ramana," I suggested. And so we found ourselves driving towards Arunachala.

It was sunset. Crimson and amethyst. As the sun started sinking, a blood-red orb of life into the west, a Golden Jasmine moon rose in the east, and standing in the centre of it all, like a gigantic incense burner of the Gods, stood the deep blue, dark rock-cut hill of Arunachala. And from its summit smoke and fire issued. It reminded me of a hissing volcano. But it was instead an annual Festival. Tons of butter, poured into a gigantic vessel, were set alight and this was what one saw as one approached the hill. There were a myriad of torches and lanterns lighting the side of the mountain, all looking like giant fireflies. The blue magic of the night closed upon us, yet, with her calm camphor beauty of pale ivory the moon rose like some wraith, shedding her soft diffused light on this scene, so primordial in its ritual.

With the great Yogi, Hanumantha Swamiji

The author with his dog Simon

Nijinski and Ram Gopal 1948

There were countless pilgrims. And no wonder. To this
sacred hill, as old as time, was attached the 'Enlightened One'
a direct descendant of the great masters of spiritual attainment
for which India has been a chosen land of manifestation. Then
there was the fatiguing walk up and down this boulder-strewn
hill, where it seemed that each rock had within it a hidden
spirit.

And then we came into the hall and were with several
others from the Hill of the Holy Beacon who had come to
get the *darshan* of the great sage himself. As he reclined
there, his face fanned by attendants, velvety peace and
love emanated from his two dark, starry eyes. Yes, he did
look like my father. But Maharishi was father to thousands.
I fell into a state of silence. I closed my eyes. And I had the
feeling of communicating in the silence of my spirit with
this great sage.

His whole philosophy is summed up in his own words:
'Who am I?' Accordingly, the pure Self is not realised unless
the mind subsides. Mind is nothing but a bundle of thoughts,
and the first and foremost of all thoughts is the primal
I-Thought. Therefore, it is only through the enquiry 'Who
am I?' that the mind subsides. To keep the mind constantly
turned within and to abide thus in the Self is alone Self-
Enquiry. That which is Bliss is verily the Self. Bliss and the
Self are one and identical. And that alone is real. Not even
in one of the countless objects of the world is there anything
that can be called happiness. This phenomenal world is
nothing but thought. When the mind is free from thought it
enjoys the bliss of the Self. The Mind of the Enlightened
One never exists apart from the Self Absolute of Brahmin.
God and Guru are one. He that has earned the grace of the
Guru shall undoubtedly be saved and never forsaken. But the
disciple, for his part, should follow the path shown by the
Master. Likes and dislikes, love and hatred are equally to be

M

eschewed. It is not proper to let the mind rest often on the objects and events of mundane life. If the Ego subsides, all else will also subside. The deeper the humility with which we conduct ourselves, the better it is for us. Everything that is offered to others is really an offering to oneself. Not to desire anything extraneous to oneself is *vairagya* or dispassion. Not to give up one's hold on the Self is *jnana* or Enlightenment. Thus, *vairagya* and *jnana* are really one and the same. Pledged to *vairagya*, every aspirant must dive deep into himself and realise the precious *atman*, the Self Absolute."

I had also read the life and works of an extraordinary thinker and philosopher, Sri Aurobindo, whose *ashram* hermitage is in Pondicherry. His background and early life, like that of India's present Prime Minister Nehru, were strongly influenced by the teaching and influences of England. Until the age of five, English and Hindustani were the only languages he could speak. At the age of seven, he was taken by his father (a man who was all for the British way of education) to England, and along with his two brothers was put under the guardianship of an English clergyman and his wife.

"In no circumstances or conditions do I want any of my children to associate, meet or become friendly with any Indians. It is for this reason that I have brought them all the way from India to your great country. Your system of education is unlike anything we have in India or are ever likely to have. And I want them to absorb completely and soak themselves into the culture, traditions and literature of your way of thinking"—thus spoke his father who was a proud, purposeful Bengali gentleman. Nobody stood in his way, and he dominated his family with a will of steel.

Naturally the Victorian-bred English clergyman and his wife were only too happy to 'save the souls' of these three boys! And it was only after he was twenty that Aurobindo saw India again.

How similar was the upbringing of the present Prime Minister, Nehru. His father, one of the fieriest of Indians, with an all powerful personality given to blinding flashes of temper when obstacles stood in his way, was determined that the young Nehru should also be given a completely Westernised education, which was what actually happened. And I strongly believe that the practical education and discipline of the sobering English weather and method of schooling had a lot to do with the very positive attitude of 'action' rather than inaction in the lives of these two great men. Posterity has yet to write the final word.

I am constantly asked whether Western people are able to assimilate and study *Yoga* successfully. Let me give you the opinion of Krishna Prem, a Westerner, who has made a sincere study of Aurobindo's Integral *Yoga* :

"Recently the psychologist Jung, in the course of some sympathetic and interesting comments on a Chinese Taoist book, found occasion to animadvert against those Westerners who practise Eastern *Yogas*. It is quite true that much, probably most, of the so-called *Yoga* practice indulged in by Westerners is foolish and misguided. That is, however, not because it is 'Eastern' in origin, but because it is not pursued for the right reason. *Yoga* is to be undertaken for the sake of truth itself, for the sake of what the Buddha termed 'unshakeable deliverance of heart'. To practise it, as many do, out of curiosity, in search of new sensations, or in order to gain psychic powers, is a mistake which is punished with futility, neurosis or worse. None should seek initiation into the mysteries from unworthy motives, or disaster will surely result . . . the path is not a pure Oriental one, having, as Jung would say, no roots in a Western psyche, but is something universal to be found in all traditions and fit to be trodden by anyone who has the will to do it."

Aurobindo was early inspired with the ancient *Yoga* and teachings of the 'Bhagavad Gita', or Song of God. But he attempted in his lifetime to go a step further in his Integral *Yoga*. That step further took him over a decade of ceaseless endeavour and experiment.

"I think I can say that I have been testing day and night for years upon years, more scrupulously than any scientist, his theory or method on the physical plane," he writes in his Letters in Volume II, page 69. "To see Truth does not depend on a big intellect or a small intellect. It depends on being in contact with the Truth and the mind silent and quiet to receive it," he writes in Volume IV. "Europeans throughout the centuries have practised with success disciplines which were akin to Oriental *Yoga* and have followed, too, ways of the inner life which came to them from the East. Especially since the introduction of Christianity, Europeans have followed its mystic disciplines which were one in essence with those of Asia, however much they may have differed in forms, names and symbols."

It is not the Hindu outlook or the Western that fundamentally matters in *Yoga*, meaning 'union with God' but the psychic turn, and anyone who has read of the austerities and ascetisism of Saint Francis of Assisi and that of St. Theresa of Avila, will not contest that their discipline and subjecting of the body equals that of any of the great known Indian sages from the times of Milarepa, the Tibetan *Yogi*, to that of Ramana Maharishi and Sri Aurobindo himself. In Sri Aurobindo's *The Human Cycle*, he sums up exactly what I believe in myself. He says: "They will adopt in its heart of meaning the inward view of the East which bids man seek the secret of his Destiny and Salvation within, but also they will accept, though with a different turn given to it, the importance which the West rightly attaches to life and to the making the best we know and can attain in the General life."

I can profess that the teachings of these masters, of whose work I have tried to give you a glimpse in its 'essential spirit' have given me and continue to illuminate me with hope and courage and strength. During my wanderings in the Himalayas, in Benaras, Hardwar, Rajputana, Central and Southern India and Ceylon I have come upon, in my search for that 'Needle of Truth in a Haystack' much that was false. . . . But I also had the great exaltation of Spirit in finding many worthwhile moments of 'Inward Illumination'. I would have to write a whole book to tell you about the great experiences I had with so many Holy Ones and seekers, perhaps that must wait till the appointed time.

As these great masters distilled from the continual labour of their Spirit in seeking out and finding moments of Truth, which is God, I have also sought to reveal and find exactly those very moments of 'self-realisation' through the Dance. Dressed as a God, wearing the head-dresses of those Gods, moving to the rhythm of the stringed *veena*, sobbing flute and softly clashing cymbals, and the chanting of my musicians, I step out of the dimension of this Earth, this Time, for I dance in tune to the Infinite.

CHAPTER THIRTEEN

End of the War—and After

THE war had ended. Or had it? However, technically it had. I wondered if it ever would. To me a material war was always an action following the 'inner' turmoil in man of ignorance hatred and lust for power which really had its seat and birth within the heart of man and his fellow-beings. And again the old wheels of Buddhist thought started turning in my mind "Until bitterness, hatred, selfishness and all the evil lusts are weeded out from within the heart of mankind, until then, only then would there be no war in an outward manifestation of bloodshed". But would mankind ever reach that state of evolution, spiritually and mentally, to achieve a lasting peace? I doubted it then, and writing today I doubt it still more. Perhaps it's all part of some design of God, for the destiny of this world, this little basement mud ball planet of His, to make both the relative forces of Darkness and Light hold sway in an eternal battle of continual strife.

What momentous changes had come about in India! She was on the threshold of Freedom and one tremulously wondered if she would bear that responsibility without the loss of blood. If one had only been 'seer' enough to visualise that soon Gandhi would be assassinated by a Hindu, and that the great brotherhood of Hindu and Moslem would be bursting into a blood bath denying the ancient scriptural and spiritual teachings of the sacred Masters and their great teachings.

I had been the first artist in India and Asia to offer my services for ENSA, and had had untold difficulty dancing in this most disorganised 'organisation' for bringing entertainment to the Indian and British troops. It is amusing now, but was not at that time, to find that a whole company of my dancers and musicians would arrive at a town to be told by the Commanding Officer that they were not informed of our arrival from G.H.Q. and were not expecting us! Innumerable incidents such as this ended in my going to Eric Dunstan, the head of ENSA, and terminating my contract.

"Temperament, old boy, temperament. All you artists whether western or eastern are alike," said Dunstan, running long nervous hands through his white hair, his pale face and blue eyes flaming with anger.

"Temperament be damned," I snapped back. "What the devil am I supposed to do, arriving not once, but time and again at various stations, to be told that neither food, board nor lodgings had been arranged for us in advance as they were not informed of our arrival? *Yogis* may eat grass or leaves, but we hard-working artists on the stage need basic shelter and food. In any case here is the contract and I have had enough of ENSA. Good-bye."

With a shudder of relief I walked out of the office, thankful at last not to face groups of Indian artists all confronting me like angry wolves and bleary-eyed from work, looking angrily at me, as if I were to blame for the ineptitude of ENSA!!!

My mother had passed on, father had followed closely after, the old house had lost its spirit and become rather like a tomb. Yes, I would follow my intuition. I must go on now, move away. Where? London of course. Where else? All my background had been with English friends, teachers and memories, those wonderful pre-war 1939 memories of the Aldwych where I had danced for the first time.

On Wednesday, July 2nd, 1947, I sailed for England.

Everything had changed in England, in beloved London. Everything but the spirit of the people of this great city. If it had been badly bombed, and the war had left its visible and invisible scars, these would heal quicker here than in other countries and people affected by the war, because of the incredible courage, humour and quenchless spirit of the English. The theatre had boomed during the war, and now as before there was a season of ballet. De Basil and the Sadlers Wells Theatre too, I remember. And it was at Covent Garden that I met, fat and smiling Dr. Braunsweg, the impresario. "You sign contract with me. I make seasons London, Paris, America, all right?" 'All right' meant that after our lawyers had satisfied each other, Braunsweg and I had agreed to work together.

Over a year later, in 1948, the Government of India accepting an offer to send my company to New York had to include Braunsweg, and it was during his visit there through me that Markova and Dolin signed to form what Markova had called the 'Festival Ballet' that exists today alongside the Sadlers Wells Ballet as representative of Diaghilev's influence on Ninette de Valois, Markova and Dolin in English dancing.

On September 17th, 1947, I was asked to dance at the reopening of the Indian section of the Victoria and Albert Museum. What a privilege! On one of the occasions during this series of lectures I remember hearing the voice of Arnold Haskell, saying a few words introducing me to the public. What wonderful words, how inspiring! All those seven years of endless work with my great dance masters, my pupils and my nation-wide tours in India, had perhaps merited the nectar of Arnold's voice as I heard him say: "I count it a great honour and also a pleasure to introduce Mr. Ram Gopal. I cannot pretend to any deep understanding of Indian dancing and art that was venerable centuries before the ballet was conceived, but I can appreciate an exceptional artist in any branch of the Dance, and Ram Gopal is an exceptional artist. It was a particularly good idea to introduce a living work of art to this museum building for there are centuries of sculpture in the body of Ram Gopal. The works of art at which I have just been looking explain his dancing, and his dancing makes them live. Mr. Gopal, I think I can take it upon myself to greet you, not only on behalf of the audience here this afternoon, but also in the name of the vast public in this country who love the art of the Dance and those who practise it."

And to that touching tribute of Haskell's, I danced. Shevanti, my beautiful partner danced too. But to me most important of all was the fact that the spark I had kindled in 1939 had been rekindled again after a lapse of seven years— that divine spark of the artist, linking through the mute rhythmic language of the dance, the Oneness of the East and West, expressing itself, albeit differently, but basically through the spirit, commuting and sharing the vision of the 'inner spirit' of Art. And that to me was all important.

Shortly after, there were London seasons of several weeks of complete Indian ballet with my tireless group of artists, at the Prince's Theatre, the Saville, the Adelphi, and the Cambridge. There were also for me nostalgic memories of 1939, of the Aldwych and the Vaudeville Theatres, where I had had such wonderful successes. These post-war seasons were even better, but tinged with sadness—the strange depressing feeling of something once tasted but now gone for ever. But then I was a dancer, and Siva that God of Creation, Preservation and Destruction was a dancer too, and so I must dance in the now, plan and create in the future. That was one of the precepts of spiritual teachings of the Masters that I had been lucky to acquire in the Himalayas, Tibet and certain centres in India notably Arunachala and Sri Aurobindo's in the south.

One morning my telephone rang. It was Braunsweg. "I have contract. You come? I come? All right, I come, I meet you hotel. I have contract for Scandinavia, we must make artistic 'sings' there, big ballet, exotic ballet, we make success, I coming now. . . ." He rang off, and I felt as breathless as Braunsweg sounded. A little later he outlined his plans. We had a contract at the Cirkus Theatre in Stockholm and possibly if successful there, all those northern countries.

There was of course another reason why I was eager to visit Stockholm particularly. I wanted to walk up the stairs to a fourth floor flat and look into a four-room apartment. The address? 32 Blekingegatan. It would be a breathless experience for me, like visiting the abode or *ashram*, sacred place of some saint. Now you will wonder who lived there and why I should want above everything to see this place? I will tell you. A little baby was born there in 1906 on September 18th, Greta Lovisa Gustafsson, and she became the divine star of my childhood days and first glimpse into the movie-houses of my home town where bills on the cinemas carried her name—Greta Garbo. Those lotus-shaped eyes, those unbelievable lashes, that fabulous mouth so filled with sensual promise and yet pregnant with spiritual secrets, and that profile, matchless in its perfection, with the flowing liquid grace of her movements on the screen . . . this was Vedic magic, every hymn that the sages wrote to Lakshmi, Goddess of Beauty, Saraswati Goddess of Learning, and Parvati, that sensual wife of Siva, all these and every other distilled dream of my boyhood were incarnated in this swan called Garbo. She was as silent as the wonderful images of the Goddesses in the temples where I haunted and meditated and drowsed, and as communicative through that very potent silence itself, for my first vision of this magic called Garbo occurred in the days of the silent films. . . . Years earlier, in 1938, I had met in Hollywood Mercedes De Acosta. We had become very close friends, and still remain so. Our main interest then as now was discussing the Sage of Arunachala, a spiritual way of life, and . . . Garbo.

In due course the company, the biggest Indian company ever to appear in Stockholm, Sweden and the surrounding Scandinavian countries, opened in the Cirkus Theatre in Stockholm, situated near some public gardens. I remember the Castle Hotel in Nybrogatan, next to the Drammatens Teatern, the great theatre which had produced so many famous actors of the Swedish stage and screen, most notable amongst them Josta Eckman. . . . A Swedish friend said to me: "Garbo is a female counterpart of Josta Eckman, he was the greatest ever, in beauty, dramatic power, range, he had everything and he died some years ago, a tragic figure."

There was the usual press conference, but with this difference. I noticed that the Swedish press and those few artists who had been present at the reception to welcome us were extremely handsome and had a strange beauty unlike the general run of people in other European countries I had visited.

In and out of all this excitement, for me at any rate, the rotund figure of Braunsweg rolled about with gleeful eyes and an increasing girth line. "You make artistic 'sings' best . . . we make success, moo-ney plenty moo-ney, we make, then we go everywhere . . ." and with more splutterings, in the most humorous English ever spoken, Braunsweg would circle away, with his continual gesticulating and rolling gait. I knew then that the advance bookings must have been very good, for Braunsweg's gleaming eyes confirmed the fact, as

well as his throwing himself with all his great energy, enthusiasm and knowledge of the theatre, into making this
first season a success.　And as far as I had seen till then, he
was the most energetic and kindly of European impresarios
I had known.

Tired, pleasantly tired and drowsy, I had stretched a hand
out to the bell beside my bed, and rung for a hall porter to
bring up all the morning Stockholm papers.　How thought-
less of me!　I could not read a word of what they thought the
morning after our show.　But the morning after an opening
night was not a time for thought, it was an automatic action,
as it is with all artists from America to Japan, to see "what
the press and public think. . . ."　When an imposing bunch
of papers arrived for me I pressed the button again . . . would
the translator please come up at once from the office.　I had
to know something!!!!

"The critics are unanimous . . . extraordinary.　We are a
very cold people . . . they don't usually, they have never . . .
but this is fantastic . . ." my Swedish interpreter from the
office below went on.

"For God's sake, my dear friend . . . read to me, tell me
what you mean . . . go on translate something. . . . Oh, it
doesn't matter if the translation is not exact . . . just give me
the gist of it," I said, excited beyond words and pale with
fright.

"All right I will do my best, but forgive me my English is
bad.　Here is the *Svensk Damtidnig* of May 1948:

> "Many world famous dancers have honoured our country
> with their visit.　But there is nothing that can be compared
> to Ram Gopal and his Indian dancers and never has any-
> thing like it been seen on the Swedish stage before. . . ."

"Here is an extract from *Aftontidningen* . . .

"It is unbelievable what Ram Gopal is able to express with his hands and eyes. . . .

"And another one here, Mr. Gopal!" my friend went on, "and this is from the *Morgontidningen* . . .

"And here is something from the *Expressen* . . .

"And here yet another, *Ny Dag* . . .

"Shall I go on there are many more?" went on my interpreter friend. . . . "There is another one here and another and another. . . ."

"Thanks," I said. "Whew, that is really better than a glass of champagne in the morning. Every time you know, every time I dance I say, 'This is for God, and for the Highest,' and yet I am so curious and so weak that I just love to know what the public thinks, and the critics. Of course I am not getting vain, but I think to myself if I can get this response by 'giving' to the audience from India to Stockholm, and Paris to Tokyo, and criss-cross the world again as many times to remember where I have carried the Indian Dance, then well . . . let me work harder and give better and better and more the next time. Yes, that's it. . . . Give of the highest and the best within myself, always, every time with every expression, gesture and movement to an audience whether it be one or a thousand, but give of the last ounce of concentration and love from within . . . without."

Then there was a nervous tap on my door. Braunsweg came in purple with glee with his Chinese fat Buddha expression, followed by the handsome company manager, Michael Rouse, and Kay Ambrose . . . all congratulations, all smiles. I was so amused that I thought: 'What would their expressions have been had we flopped?'

We greeted one another, laughed and drank coffee. Later, months later, we toured Finland, Denmark and Norway, and all the main cities and the provinces of those strange cold northern countries of handsome and beautiful people.

I had not forgotten to go to two places. One was Garbo's birthplace, 32 Blekingagatan on the South Side. The other? The grave of Mauritz Stiller where I went to pay silent homage to his genius and the fact that he had given the world the great vision of truth and beauty and drama I had perceived in Garbo, his creation. I scattered some yellow flowers and roses on his grave, and Mimi Pollack, a director and actress friend of Garbo's, was with me. Crowds waved farewell to us as our train steamed out of the station at Stockholm . . . and I cried at having to say good-bye to that great, wonderful, city which had loved me as much as I had fallen in love with its beauty, tradition and people.

CHAPTER FOURTEEN

Return to America

AFTER my first impact with the Swedish public, and a
public which saw me in 1948, not only in Stockholm
but all the major cities of Sweden, I toured Oslo and
the rugged beauty of the countryside towns in Norway,
followed by Finland, which still had an air of romantic
Czarist Russia clinging about it, especially Helsinki. Here
was one of the most colourful, remote and picturesque towns
I had ever seen. Those cold sapphire blue Northern Lights,
the churches and houses, the cobbled streets, and the Svensk
Teatern where we danced, with the unbelievable enthusiasm
of the public there for the remote dances of India, all these
were an unforgettable experience.

Since that first tour in those northern countries, I have
danced there many times, each occasion confirming the first
impression made on me of great friendliness and hospitality
and genuine interest to know something of mysterious India
and her peoples and arts through our Indian dances.

In Copenhagen, too, I had wandered all over the city. In
the museum attached to the great Opera Dance Theatre I
found memories of Lucille Grahn and Taglioni. In the theatre,

more alive than ever today is the very spirit of the Romantic Ballet in its purest tradition. I saw *Swan Lake*, *Giselle*, *and La Sylphide*.

After a tour of Scandinavia and Switzerland, we were invited to represent our own country at the request of Nehru the Prime Minister of India, at an international festival in America. We opened at the New York City Centre in October, and gave a series of performances which were presented by the great Sol Hurok, whose name was often more exciting to the public than the performances, in that Hurok, having presented Pavlova, Duncan, Challiapine and other great artists down to Shankar before and after the war, was the undisputed king of ballet impresarios, both from the West and East. Memorable from that 1948 visit to America is the review of Cecil Smith of the *Daily Express*. He wrote at that time for *Musical America* and later came over to London where he wrote some of the most constructively critical reviews I have ever read.

"Ram Gopal's appearances were arranged under the auspices of the Government of India. . . . Our only other distinguished visitor from India has been Uday Shankar, whose dances, however beautiful they may have been, were scarcely more representative of traditional Indian art than, say, Gustav Holst's choral settings of texts from the *Rig Veda*. Because Shankar developed a style which was artificially restrained, small in scope and limited in vocabulary, the assumption has been widespread in the United States that Indian dancing is a careful, almost a precious, form of art with little theatrical flair, and virtually no element of exhibition. The falsity of this assumption was demonstrated from the start by the vigour and dramatic impact of Ram Gopal and his dancers, their magnificent, wide use of space, and their unhesitating use of devices to startle the

observer, to move his emotions, and to keep his attention
fresh. . . . With no adequate standard of comparison, it
might seem difficult at first glance to assess the quality of
Ram Gopal's dancing and that of his company. But great
dancing is unmistakable whatever its idiom. There is
nothing esoteric or withdrawn about Ram Gopal; he is not
afraid to establish a rapport with his audience, or to let
them see the technical difficulty as well as beauty of his
art and nobody left the City Centre without realising that
he had seen a practitioner supreme in his field. Ram Gopal
has opened a tremendous new world of dance and music to
us and he is sure to develop a large and permanent follow-
in this country."

So tempered and seasoned a review coming from *Musical
America*, written by a connoisseur of music and dance, both in
London and New York, only gave me one further ambition,
and that was to carry the art from the fields of Europe to the
vast continent of America and spread a further love and
understanding of my country. I visited America later in 1954,
to attend the summer session of Jacob's Pillow, invited by
the great pioneer of American dance, Ted Shawn, who with
Ruth St. Denis, had done so much to further the cause of
concert dancing in the States. Jacob's Pillow was a revela-
tion of concentrated work, in an ideal woodland setting, with
the white spirit of Shawn. Here dancers of all the known and
created styles taught, learned, danced and lectured, side by
side. The green lawns were filled with Russian, Spanish,
Hindu, Modern American and Mexican dance groups and
artists. The air of informality, the cabin huts of the students,
and the whole atmosphere in 1954 were pervaded for me
with an atmosphere of devotion. Ted Shawn always spoke to
the vast audiences who filled the theatre that year, and alongside my appearances there, the Celtic Ballet Group from

N

Scotland scored a sensational success. Shawn in his talk before
the curtain rose, when he spoke all dressed in white, became
a mixture of Peter Pan, Nijinsky and the youthful spirit of
America. What an invaluable contribution this great pioneer
and artist is making to the dance-loving public of the world.
All nationalities mingle, all arts are seen, discussed and dis-
sected, and all in the friendly, natural setting of the unforgettable Jacob's Pillow.

The only places, after America, to move me with their age-
old traditions and beauty were Istanbul and Ankara. In 1949
Turkey was as beautiful as a fairy-tale city and our ballet made
there a deeper impression than in any other country in the
Middle East. Unfortunately, after Turkey I returned to
India, and instead of concentrating on renovating costumes,
dances and technique, I was tempted to embark on a catas-
trophic tour that included South India and Ceylon. The
'business partners' of the business deal vanished with large
slices of the box office takings, and in the end I was, as so
often in India, left without financial resources. In 1950, I
was back again in London. A little later, I had seasons at the
Adelphi and the Cambridge theatres which were very
successful.

In all these tours I had seen a lot of Russian, Spanish and
European ballet. But the most vivid American dance personality was Martha Graham, who looked like an Earth
Goddess with fierce and yet kindly eyes, and a face of unusual strength, bone structure and depth. Her style incorporated Russian, Wigman and Kathakali in its violence and
gave me the impression of roots that were violently seeking
an outlet. As a scientist, experimenting with new forms of
rhythmic dance, she is supreme; supreme that is, outside the
traditional perfection of the Russian ballet and the still greater
traditions of Hindu dancing. But each age has its chosen high
priests and priestesses. Perhaps Graham is carrying the torch

of Isadora Duncan. Perhaps, too, she is representative of the restless, generous, sexual American spirit of passion and childlike innocence, for to me her style is the reflection of the spirit of the New World.

CHAPTER FIFTEEN

My Troupe and My Work

ORGANISING a troupe in India presents many difficulties. First the Indian dancer and musician is a
highly individual personality: tense, moody, difficult,
jealous and often unco-operative in the extreme, yet de-
manding and lazy in turn. I was very fortunate when selecting
my present company, composed from among the greatest
available talent in India today, in finding not only first-rate
technicians but also educated men and women to work with.

Shevanti, that exquisite dancer of great beauty and a fluid
grace so very pronounced in her Manipuri and Kathak dances,
was one of my first pupils and partners. Arnold Haskell re-
counts how Menaka introduced Shevanti to him like some
priceless jewel during his visit to India before the war on his
way to Australia. He spent a brief time there where Madam
Menaka, a pioneer of Hindu dancing, entertained Haskell and
members of the Russian Ballet in Bombay. Shevanti was
Menaka's favourite dancer, and later, when she joined me and
I personally trained her in her Tanjore temple dances and
other items, she became not only my favourite pupil but
from 1944 onwards my leading partner and soloist. She has a
superb technique, with an unbroken fluidity of movement I

have not seen equalled. In her Tanjore dances she has a bewitching grace and charm that captivate. Now she is happily
married to Rajeshwar Rao, a lithe, panther-like pupil of mine
from Secunderabad. They live in a miniature palace in Hyderabad and are noted for their generous hospitality and kindness to all their friends. Shevanti in 1956 was eager to return
to Europe, where I had previously introduced her and to
appear with my new company at the Edinburgh Festival. She
made a great success dancing the role of the Empress Mumtaz
Mahall alternately with Kumudini.

Kumudini was a little slip of a girl when she joined me in
1948 in London. She is married now to Rajanai Lakhia, a
musician with a great knowledge of Hindu music. They both
met through me, and are now happily blessed with a beautiful
young son, Shri Raj, whom I have nicknamed 'the Prince'.

I have seen the dance of Sitara the popular Indian film star.
I remember seeing her films from my childhood and admired
this Indian actress's vivacity on films. Having retired from
films in India, where she has been a star for nearly thirty
years, she has now devoted much time to Kathak dancing and
is popular with dance audiences in India and London. But
after seeing the superb line, lightning spins and great purity of
Kumudini's Kathak dancing, and her strict adherence to the
Jylal and Radhelal (leading maestros) schools of Kathak
dancing, I could never appreciate or tolerant the modernised
and adulterated versions of Sitara by comparison with the
matchless Kumudini.

Technically superior to Kumudini was Jai Kumari, a
tornado of rhythm and speed, the like of which I have never
seen in this style of dancing anywhere in the world. But she
danced like a perfected machine, soulless and expressionless.
And it is these very qualities of soul and expression that make
Kumudini a great dancer. She is one of the foremost dancers
of the younger generation of India today and should she stay

the cruel course of a dancer's life, she should be one of the greatest in India.

Now I come to Satyavati. I have not seen any female dancer in South India who possessed the grace, expression and plastic line of movement, aided by a vivid personality, to approach Satyavati. She learnt under the great Shankaran Namboodri, the master of Uday Shankar, and even under Shankar himself. From Namboodri she learned his most treasured secrets of expression and rhythm in Kathakali dancing, all the *lasya* (feminine) expressions. From Shankar she learned much of his own style of sinuous and graceful folk and other dances. Combining the two, Satyavati is a poem of grace on the stage, and in her Sita Apaharan, the Abduction of Sita, has scored a great success with Namboodri at the Edinburgh Festival and London seasons. Immaculate in person and dress, she has a considerable following of young pupils in Bombay, and is herself a writer of talent.

With Shevanti, Kumudini and Satyavati, three of India's greatest female dancers, I was indeed very lucky and happy to work so long and hard all those months in Bombay during my recent visit there, and then in London prior to our dancing at the Edinburgh Festival.

I had on the male side a strongly representative group of artists: Yogen Desai, that highly skilled choreographer and dancer whom I had met in 1938, now came to work with me as choreographer. He is the resident teacher at the Bharatiya Vidya Bhavan in Bombay, a theatre devoted to staging plays and dance dramas with local talent. Raman Lal, the Kathak teacher and dancer, Surendra for Manipuri dancing, Satyavan for folk dancing and Namboodri the Brahmin, from Malabar and a great actor-dancer in Kathakali dancing. I was fortunate to get Rajani Lakhia as musical director. His genius in creating the most lyrical and exquisite melodies always surprised me, and the music he created for the Taj Mahal

Ballet, the first full-length two-hour ballet ever to come out of India is a masterpiece of Indian music, in mood, theme and rhythm. Rajani can capture in a few minutes the intention of the choreographer, the rhythm of the dancers and the mood of the scene for any group or solo dance and create, almost instantly, the most beautiful music from his inexhaustible knowledge of classical Hindustani music.

I think I had best conclude this short chapter, in which I have given an outline of some of the outstanding artists who have worked with me in creating my two latest programmes *Dances of India* and *The Legend of the Taj Mahal*, by quoting from a talk I gave recently in Bombay and London, and which prefaces what I have attempted to do. Here it is:

"India has a tradition of dancing that is today, perhaps the oldest and most detailed of all existing techniques. Japan, where I had the privilege of learning from Koshiro Matsumoto for a year shortly before the war, has its gloriously preserved Kabuki. Here I discovered that Japan has some of the most sacred temple dances, originally from India, but preserved only in Japan. In the Chinese Theatre there is much in its character, make-up and style of dancing strongly reminiscent of the Kathakali dance-drama of Malabar. Bali and Java are strongly influenced by the dance of India in the enacted dramas of the Ramayana and Mahabharata, with a style of gesture and rhythmic control very similar to that in the Indian dance. Of the two, the dance dramas of Bali, where I have been are perhaps nearer in dynamism and movement, to the Kathakali of Malabar than those of any other country in the East.

"In my programme *Dances of India* you will see extracts of the four great dance schools, authentic in costume, music and style, and performed by outstanding artists. Very strongly in evidence, too, are colourful and exciting folk dances, such as the 'Rabari Ras' from Gugerat, a highly skilful dance that marks time with sticks in an ever quickening tempo. Also the 'Katchi Gori', horse dances of the north.

"On my recent tour of India, I discovered that the robust, earthy, vital and colourful folk dances have swept the cities of Delhi and Bombay with festivals of folk dancing lasting for weeks. Troupes of folk dancers and musicians, numbering as many as fifty in each group, gave some of the most wonderful dances I have yet seen. There are hundreds of folk dancing groups from all the various provinces of India, and still many more yet to be discovered, and they depict an aspect of the colour and beauty of India that equals or even surpasses, some of the classical dance styles of that ancient land.

"It was evident to me during my 1956 tour of India that the Indian public of today, used to the colourful films of the West and of India, will not support the purely technical or acrobatic feats of either the egotistic solo dancer imposing him or herself on the public for hours, or the rather slipshod groups that perform in the name of Hindu ballet. What is true of the twentieth century public in India is true of the great dance-loving public of the West, and that is that the dance, be its style Russian, Spanish, Chinese, Japanese or Hindu, has to be vital, authentic, edited and artistically presented. This I have attempted in my programme *Dances of India*.

"In my ballet *The Legend of the Taj Mahal*, I have used the classical and folk dance techniques for clothing a love story, in my opinion one of the most moving and tragic in the world of drama, and using the authentic costumes and background from the Rajput and Moghul paintings of the time, for which I have to acknowledge my indebtedness to Mr. William Archer of the Victoria and Albert Museum, in giving me access to the superb collection of pictures and material from that era of Shah Jehan.

"After having studied the traditional technique for several years with the great acknowledged masters of the Hindu Dance, Meenakshisundaram Pillai of Tanjore, and Kunju Kurup of Malabar, I find that the Hindu Dance is in danger of becoming a 'Museum Piece' rather than the means of giving beauty and truth to the world which was, and is, the main object of the Hindu Dance according to ancient treatises in Sanskrit. And it is in the 'giving' of truth and beauty, and by the using of traditional and authentic styles, that one can preserve the old and also create the new, and thus keep the Dance of India, not thousands of years old, but thousands of years young, within the tempo of life and the understanding of the people of today. And in both my programmes, *Dances of India*, and *The Legend of the Taj Mahal*, I feel I have justified the past while keeping in touch with the present."

CHAPTER SIXTEEN

New Delhi, circa *1956*

IT was ten years since I had danced at New Delhi. What would it be like? How would it look? And what sort of reception would I get there? Mrs. Pandit, India's High Commissioner in London, had assured me that the Indian Government would give me a support for both the Exhibition of Indian Art at the Edinburgh Festival and the Hindu ballet which had both been already advertised to take place that year at Edinburgh. Well, I would soon know. If I had ONLY known! My plane took off from London Airport on a very cold winter morning early in the New Year, 1956, and shortly after touched down in Paris, where Retna Cartier Bresson, my ex-dancing partner, wonderful friend, and wife of the famous photographer met me with Amala, one of the beautiful girls I had trained and who always appeared in my programmes.

"San San (her nickname for me), I wish I could dance with you again, but I have not been well. My chest. Send me some sweets, San San. Oh, and don't forget to bring me *saris* and joss sticks. I remember so well 1938 when we were in Malabar at Vallathol's Dancing Academy preparing to come to Europe with a troupe. Oh, how I wish I could come with

you! Here is something"—slipping a small box into my hands
—"and, darling San San, promise you'll write, take care of
yourself . . ." she hugged me affectionately—"and if there is
anything I can do for you let me know."

"Good-bye, Retna, and thank you for coming. I feel sad
leaving you, somehow. And you take care of yourself.
Yes, promise—I'll write. But you promise that you will
reply. God bless and remember me in your prayers. . . .
Good-bye."

The most eventful and wonderful experience of that flight,
happened at two o'clock in the morning when I saw, to the
left of the port side engines, in the darkness of the cabin, a
wonderful lightning thunderstorm. It was the most awe-
inspiring sight I have ever beheld. We had crossed Italy, and
were approaching Greece, flying over Mount Olympus, the
Mount of the Gods of Greek mythology, and for those few,
intermittent seconds during a darting spasm of lightning the
whole scene was illumined revealing the famous mountain
and the clouds and the town and even the sea. This scene
flashed before my eyes like some Morse signal from Outer
Space . . . and all my recollections and dreamy communion,
as a child, with the Greek Gods came vividly back with each
flash. Suddenly the plane trembled, and shivered, and even
rocked. And then the steward told me that all would be well,
there was a storm and we would skirt the worst part of it.
We were circling it, going to the East. One hour of drama
in the Heavens, as those Rolls-Royce engines thundered
around those dark clouds. Who knows, perhaps Zeus and
Adonis with Diana and Aphrodite were giving me a signal and
warning that they were aware of me, or perhaps with me in
what was to come. . . .

New Delhi . . . and my friends, the Chamanlalls, were
there to greet me. "You know how I hate welcoming people
as much as saying good-bye to them" . . . and, smiling like a

Queen, Helen Chamanlall added, "but you are a special friend!"

"Oh, thanks . . . it's such a thrill seeing you again since London last year. . . ." Their car sped into Delhi City and I was deposited at a central hotel somewhere near Connaught Circus . . . I was so tired, that after bidding my two friends good night I went up and sleepily signed a register and then went straight to my room and to sleep.

When I awoke I still thought I was at my flat in London . . . but it couldn't be, I was greeted for a change by a brilliant blue sky that peeped at me through the window and a bracing wintery wind, crisp, warm, invigorating. Yes this was Delhi, I was in India, my beloved wonderful homeland. And what a marvellous company I was going to get together, with the modest budget, which Mrs. Pandit assured me the Government of India would grant me for the ballet and exhibition that very same September in Edinburgh. . . .

The next few days, weeks, months wasted into each other and became grimy with depression, sadness and a certain sense of futility as far as my progress, if one could call it so, was concerned. I was fighting a battle for Indian art, with nearly twenty years of experience, toil and sweat behind me and the Government of India, in the form of the Ministry of Education in the persons of its appointed administrators, was being difficult, and that is putting it mildly. It was whispered to me by my friends that sinister forces were working over-time against me to 'sabotage' every effort of mine to dance at the Edinburgh Festival. The 'saboteurs' I was told, were other Indian dancers who wanted the honour of dancing abroad, and who were seeing to it that those with whom they could pull strings, that is their friends in the Government of India, were doing all they could, in fact, to prevent me from dancing there with any support from the Government of India or any other source if that were at all possible!

At first I did not know what to make of the rumours.
Surely they could not be jealous of me and stoop to such low
levels, and even so, was not the Government of India aware
of my work, culturally, and as an artist, in the goodwill
created for India by my dancing as an unofficial Cultural Ambassador in the East, West and Turkey and other countries
eager to know and learn something about India? Here is an
extract from my New Delhi diary of March, 1956.

Monday. 10.30. Appointment with Official at Ministry of
Education.

"Good morning."

"Good morning, Ram Gopal," said my friend, "do sit down.
Tea? Coffee? Cigarette?"

"Thanks no. You see I've already been some time in Delhi.
Time is so short and I do want to get working on the project
of representing, in the best possible manner, like the Chinese,
Japanese and Russians, an aspect of our arts, so eagerly looked
forward to at the Edinburgh Festival. . . ."

"So you think it's a good idea dancing at this, what did you
call it . . . er . . . Edinburgh Festival?" His face clouded.

"Wonderful idea in fact. I've been working, planning, and
dreaming about it for years, and now comes the chance to do
this for our country at the Festival. I'll bring the greatest ever
credit to India, and surpass anything I've ever done previously.
You'll see. . . . Oh, and yes," I added, unfastening the zip of
my leather case, "here are the modest budgets . . . two full
programmes . . . entirely different, that is two hours of completely different evenings of our Dance and Drama. . . ."

I looked up to find that my words might have been spoken
to the wind. There was a vacant look in the eyes of this
official, whose gaze was rivetted on some cows that were
eating grass on a lawn outside the office. There was an icy
silence. What could be wrong? I asked myself. One would
have thought that there was something sinful and wrong about

wanting to dance and create beauty through the medium of the Dance!

A sigh, like an escaping hiss of volcanic steam issuing from a fissure, came from the man across the table. "Ram Gopal, I will be very brutal with you. Very frank, that is my nature . . . you see WE are not interested in Edinburgh or elsewhere . . . couldn't care less, tear up your contract, throw it away. . . ." His eyes blazed at me through two narrowing slits of an angry face. I sat back stunned, swallowing hard.

"What do we care about England, the West, Edinburgh. You come and dance here in Delhi, dance around India. Go to China, go anywhere you like, but not THERE . . ." A pause as he gulped, some long since dead pang of his obvious European education probably trying to assert itself like some ghost behind that ghastly pallor that contorted his bigoted face . . . and then the full venom, anger, prejudice and narrow-minded bigotry of this petty official from the Ministry of Education asserted itself. When he had finished he said: "Have some tea . . . you are a great, a very great artist . . . come on . . . have tea. . . ." Behind this pretended politeness came a look of satisfaction in those beady eyes.

I felt a hurricane of indignant fury and pent-up rage well up within me. What to do now? Still myself, take deep breaths, remember the words and teachings of Shri Aurobindo and the sage of Arunachala? Or else as Krishna says to Arjuna when confronted with an enemy, fight? I turned on him like a flash, and opened up a blast, eyes blazing and head hot I felt myself release my anger and my point of view.

"You have been frank, very frank and outspoken, now let me tell you something. I, too, am a very, very frank person. Are you aware of the hard work, years of service to the cause of the Dance in India both here and abroad, and the suffering that I have gone through . . . have you heard of what I have done and what glory I've brought proudly to India through my art of dancing? And is this the greeting that I get on my first visit in ten years to Delhi? Dance in India? I'd love to do that, only I don't want to be cheated like I was by absconding impresarios, so-called, who landed me into £12,000 worth of deficits. . . . Where are the theatres for the artists? Where are the impresarios? Look at China, Russia, Japan. An artist is given every encouragement. People like you can be manufactured, people like me have to be born . . . born do you hear me, to dance!"

After that I said that I had not come to beg for anything personal, it was for the cause of Art and India, and I had come to ask as an Indian and an artist. Politics were not my line, never interested me, never could.

"I'll tell you something . . ." my friend went on, a bit shaken that he had got a blast hotter than he had given and surprised at my flow of eloquence. "I'll do all I can to stop you from getting any help whatever from the Government, and in every other way. . . ."

"Do your worst . . . if that's what you are here for and thank God you're not representative of the rest of India . . . do your worst . . . in fact, go to the devil . . ." and with that I got up and walked out.

I had heard that Mrs. Pandit was due in Delhi, that was a great relief. Something would surely happen now. She arrived . . . I phoned and phoned and finally saw her one morning.

". . . I am doing all I can . . . but there are difficulties . . . they think your budget is a lot of money . . . too much in fact . . ." she said.

"But they spent twice that amount of money recently in sending a 'Cultural Delegation' to China, and I am asking finally for just half that amount, surely, that's not so much. . . . Just look how much the Sadlers Wells, the Bolshoi

Ballet and other companies like the Chinese get for their ballets . . . even Yugoslavia sent two big aeroplanes loaded full . . . such a small country but what a budget for art and artists. . . ."

"I'll do all I can . . ." were the disheartening words with which I left Mrs. Pandit. She was very busy I knew that. Anybody in her position would be. But I wasn't making any headway. And ballets cannot be created in a few days, it would take me months and months of endless rehearsals. . . . Time was my enemy now . . . what would I do?

I was disconsolate . . . I was worried and I was in a bad state of nerves. I wished I could remember the ancient teachings and the great truths of Arunachala and Sri Aurobindo, those two great sages of modern India. But I was facing time . . . and time was slipping by and the months were slipping closer and closer to the Edinburgh Festival. . . . What was I going to do, what could I do?

"I know what, dear Ram, let's go and see the Taj by moonlight. You've seen it before. But come, we'll get a car, and we'll go, tomorrow morning, and we'll see the Taj and speak to the spirit of Shah Jehan and Mumtaz Mahal and tell them, ask them to help us. Also you must come to the Pearl Tomb set in white marble in the red sandstone fort of Fatehpur Sikhri, and there we will make a vow at the tomb of the great holy man who procured sons for a great Moghul Emperor. If he procured sons for him, surely he will give us blessings to see our 'child' the Taj come to life. Of course, it will have to be a miracle . . . but let's try and believe in miracles. What? Exasperating? Of course the whole thing is mad, and the people are mad, and the Ministry of Education are crazy to ignore and neglect you." This was Frieda Harris, my dear friend, speaking.

And so one evening the pale ivory pearl dream that is the Taj rose in the moonlight, shimmering and wraithlike to

'commune with us' in spirit, after we had made vows at the
Mother of Pearl Shrine, set in ivory at Fatepur Sikhri.

I left Delhi, sad, bitter and disillusioned. I went to
Bombay, and there Shevanti, Kumudini, Rajani Lakhia and
Satyavati met and discussed plans in their homes and the home
of my very dear friend and hostess Champak Khanna. They
would go on working together and, somehow, in every
possible way we would win through. But how? And where
would the money come from? My dwindling resources were
now down to nothing. But they worked on and on in the
terrible humid heat of Bombay. I flew twice to Ceylon,
having been promised financial aid from both the Government and private backers. Twice I was disappointed. I went
to Bangalore, scattered flowers on my mother's grave, and
wept and prayed. I went to see the Goddess Gaurie, that
masterpiece in a shrine outside Bangalore where a Holy Sage,
since passed over, had initiated me in so much wisdom and
Truth. From Bangalore I flew back to Hyderabad, and thence
on to Bombay. My mind was made up. A great calm and a
cool acceptance of the inevitable had descended upon me. I
would return to England.

"All of you work hard every single day and noon and night.
Do what you can to the utmost of your capacity. Soon you'll
hear from me one way or the other," I told my little faithful
band of artists in Bombay. "I'll fly to London and see what
can be done from there."

And so I found myself sailing over Mount Olympus, one
noon, and I remembered the dark lightning thunderstorm on
my way out to India, only this time the sky was blue and
there was no storm, all was sunny, coldly clear as a summer's
day. Perhaps that was an omen!

My thoughts wandered over the time I had just spent in
India. I wondered why the Government of India, who had
asked me to represent them in New York and Turkey, had

o

suddenly decided not to help me for dancing at the Edinburgh Festival? Surely the pettiness of that official I had had
the misfortune to meet would not affect the decision of the
bigger powers in Delhi?

One advantage of my stay in India was that I was able to
review the dances and the state of the theatre and cinema in
India, and I was appalled by most of what I had seen of so-
called Indian dancing. I had seen a few unspeakably vulgar
exhibitions of so-called Kathak dancing by a male and female.
Compared to Jai Kumari, Kartik and Kumudini, they had
seemed not only brash, but unforgivable, for they incorporated
the Kathakali technique, instruments and expression. The
chenda and *madallam*, two magnificent sounding drums, were
used in close unison with a saxophone and the North Indian
instruments for these so-called parodies of Kathak dancing.
Worst of all, critics, again self-styled, had permitted these
abortive exhibitions of dancing to take place alongside such
superb and serious performers as Balasaraswati, that supreme
female exponent of Bharata's 'Dasi Attam' or courtesan
dance of Tanjore. . . .

There were sincere artists, though they were few and far
between, but there was a great deal of rumbling frustration
from the few artists I had met against the exhibitions of the
many who were flooding the market with their cheap and
shoddy recitals. Shankar had left Delhi in a huff, under-
standably so. And without either Shankar or Ram Gopal,
what I wondered would, *could* happen to the Dance in India
to which both of us had devoted a lifetime of love, devotion
and dedication? Was all our invaluable experience, gleaned
in India and abroad with regard to the theatre of the world,
to go without due recognition, and without any opportunity
of passing on our knowledge to the serious minded younger
artists? The time, perhaps, I thought, then as now, was not
yet. One day . . . perhaps.

The heavy mists through which we were flying were now disappearing. The sun was shining, the setting sun golden and red . . . and below me I caught my first glimpse again, as so often before, of England. My heart grew warm with love and affection for this great land, after all I may have been born in India, but as a follower of the teachings of the Sage of Arunachala I felt I was a living human being first, and as a citizen and lover of all mankind I felt neither Eastern nor Western. The plane dipped down, racing with the crimson ball of fire that the sun had become.

Formalities over, swiftly and without fuss I was back again at home in Hyde Park Crescent. The welcome of my dog Simon, and the warmth of the room, with the loving welcome of Serafin and Greta Valentine and Audrey Homan, completed my happiness.

"I am too tired to talk. Why? What? No, my beloveds, I did not get any help from the Government. I don't suppose I shall dance at the Edinburgh Festival. I completely surrender and relax in the realisation that 'God works in many ways his wonders to perform'."

"You are certainly very calm about it all, Ram," added my friends. "What a scandal it will be if you don't appear at the Festival. Your performances are sold out, we believe. What a great pity."

"Write and tell Nehru about the 'pity' part of it. There is nothing, nothing I didn't try and do there . . . only God and a miracle can save us now."

The rest of the weeks were spent with my very dear friend Derek Patmore, a direct descendant of Coventry Patmore, the mystic and writer, in contacting Mrs. Pandit. But she was even more distant and vague. I felt she had tried to do something . . . but perhaps she was over taxed with pressing responsibilities already.

Romer Brown-Hovelt and her late mother, Eulalie, had

written some beautiful letters and verses about the effect my dancing had had on them. Browsing through an old scrap book I had come upon them. Both the Brown-Hovelts had been great supporters of my art in England. They lived in Hove. "What a pity, Ram. You've never stopped troubling about ballet ever since I can remember. Why don't you write, act in films, dance alone, it's you, and only you, the public want to see, dance solo. But company or not, you must dance again in London. I have a feeling you will." Roma Brown-Hovelt, now happily married, sounded optimistic. I didn't. Perhaps marriage had filled her life with hope and happiness. She deserved both.

I distracted myself by going to the pictures and seeing exhibitions. I met Lady Christobel Aberconway who showed me some quite priceless Manets, Cezannes and Seurats. Hers is perhaps the most beautiful house I have seen in London and she moved around the place like an ageless Muse, beautiful and youthful.

One morning, some weeks after I arrived and several days after Derek Patmore and Serozh Dadachanaji, the co-author of my book on Indian Dancing, had visited with me Mrs. Pandit, and discussed the gravity of the situation if I did not appear at the Edinburgh Festival, the telephone rang: "India House speaking. Mrs. Pandit had received £2,000 from the Government of India in response to a letter of hers. Would you come and see us as soon as possible?"

Mrs. Pandit had done all she possibly could. "You see, Ram Gopal, the very same person who has worked against you in Delhi for no reason whatever has been sabotaging everything I attempted doing in giving the West a glimpse of Indian art and life. You know why? Because I had had him removed from Washington some years ago," she explained. "This money is very, very little for the task ahead, but take it and do what you can."

Do what I could? Those words frightened me. What COULD I do with £2,000? Stage a whole full-length two-hour ballet, also arrange another programme, *Dances of India*, in addition to bringing over sixteen artists from India? To bring them by ship would be impossible, by air the only solution. After telephoning my musical director, Rajani Lakhia, in India, to stand by and encourage the artists working in the dance studio in Bombay to work still harder I decided to see my impresario, Sandor Gorlinsky, and have a talk with him. I told him exactly what the Indian Government was offering.

"£2,000. Why, that's ridiculous. The Chinese, Japanese and Russians spend fortunes on sending abroad their best artists, and is this absurd sum supposed to cover everything? Well, let's see what we can do. I tell you what, Ram. I will conclude arrangements for the Nervi Festival in Italy, then you have August for rehearsals in London, Edinburgh for a week in September and I'll fix the Royal Festival Hall for two weeks later. Later, if we're a success, there is America and there is Europe . . . in fact, there is the world. . . ." So Sandor Gorlinsky instructed his travel agents to issue the necessary tickets by air from Bombay at £125 a head, in addition to the extra costumes and curtains and rehearsals that all mounted up in the final accounts to £10,000.

And then? Little indifferent fates what now? NOW— meaning December, after the sensational successes we scored at Edinburgh, and at the new Festival Hall, London (capacity for 3,500). Looking back, it was a miracle that God alone made all this possible, merely using people, circumstances and accessories for the fulfilment of His plan. As ever, every single dancer and musician, with the others connected with the show, made their monies and profit. And I am left with a neatly stacked bunch of white paper, not Bank of England notes, but bills and debts! THAT story, as everyone knows,

is the theme song of any artiste, such as I, who is imbecile
enough to head an unsubsidised, or privately financed, Ballet
Company! But to twist the old saying a little 'Better late
than later' . . . I've learnt that this is the finale to a Herculean
struggle to group a company together and keep them working and touring, fed and paid, and taken all over India and
the West: in the end, I always have bulging scrapbooks with
rave notices and an empty bank account and writs!

However, the work has been done, the pattern followed
. . . now I look to the fields of acting, dancing and directing
pictures about India and the West with the big picture companies of the East and West, in America, England and Italy
. . . there lies salvation and the money to pay for the Hindu
Ballet of Ram Gopal!

CHAPTER SEVENTEEN

Dance of Siva

HIGH up on a peak in the Himalayas one evening I sat in complete solitude. In such a calm and peaceful atmosphere my brain was assailed by many thoughts. What is the secret of Life? Why is it that one is never taught the simple truths of the Masters and *Yogis* whose teachings would do so much to help the young avoid the great sufferings brought upon themselves in adult life?

The Great Ones about whom I have read so much and, luckier still, those few I had been privileged to meet, how near the secret of Truth and Beauty and God have they got? My thoughts continued. I was awake and yet in a trance. I could see and feel everything, but somehow it was some other spirit, from within myself that dominated me. This happens to most of us when we allow ourselves to be induced by Nature and solitude to relax in the fullest sense of that word. I looked around me at the surrounding peaks, mists and valleys, far, far below me. I heard the copper tinkle of bells, always attached to the necks of the herds, as the beasts were driven home for the approaching evening, and the blare of trumpets announcing the time for prayer and worship in the wooden temples.

Below, ahead, and above me, everything made me seem small, insignificant, nothing. And then I noticed that the immaculate white of the snow against the turquoise of the sky was beginning to take on varying and subtle changes and tones. And it was there, standing on that peak in the failing colours of dusk, as Orion, that magical star, became visible to my eyes, that my thoughts were carried to that supreme peak of this world, Mount Kailasa, abode of Shiva. That great God, the White *Yogi*, must be about to perform his sacred evening dance, the Dance of the Cosmic Rhythm of Nature, Life itself, which all the ancient Indian mystics, *rishis* and *devas*, divine beings, knew so well. Ask as I would, none of my dance teachers could tell me anything about this particular dance; and I wanted to learn how to dance it. I wanted the dance to express all the flowing, ceaseless grace of the elements of Fire, Air, Earth and Water, and somehow to convey the spirit of God in His divine mercy, taking into His arms all of the sorrow of humanity and lifting them up to heaven, restoring them to their final purity and peace.

And then, as if in a flash, I was transported, in my mind, to Mount Kailasa itself, and with a sense of exaltation, in my inner vision, or with my third eye of intuition (said to be situated in the middle of the forehead) I witnessed, amid the grandeur of the sunset in the Himalayas, this mystic dance. An old Sanskrit text says, "The Supreme intelligence dances within the Soul." That great orb of fire was sinking fast into the mists of the Cosmos, and the clouds and the mountains. The snow grew deep purple. Shaking myself out of the exalted mood that had come upon me, I walked down the pathway to my abode, situated half-way down that mountainside, in a beautiful orchard of cherry and apple trees. And that was how I created my Dance of the Setting Sun, feeling a 'presence' descend upon me, the presence of that Great *Yogi*, Siva himself, perhaps at that very moment meditating in

Kailasa itself. And when I dance the 'Sandhya Nritta Murti' The Dance of the Setting Sun, I try to reveal visibly the moments of truth that these great sages have realised. Let me tell you what a member of 'that great dark mass', the audience wrote of this dance:

"A stage muffled in black velvet, the pearl glow of one soft light . . . and within its gleam . . . his body taut with quivering muscles and lithe sinuous movements. . . . The Great Lord Siva, the Creator, at the peaceful close of the day, amidst the harmony of the sea and its waves, the four winds and the stars, arises and performs his Dance of the Setting Sun in all its fiery glory.

"A sobbing flute stirs the vapours of time. Soft, sad, insistent. From deep shadows the melody steals, its sadness a living thing. Clutching the meshes of Time it gently rolls back the æons of Time . . . fold upon fold. The melody lingers . . . it rises and it falls in rhythm with the heart beats of all time. Softly the haunting strain lingers . . . quivers as it floats into a diminuendo of tenderness. . . far, far away, it lingers . . . beyond Space, at the edge of Time.

'There was neither Existence nor non-Existence,
The Kingdom of Air nor the Sky beyond.
What was there to contain, to cover in—
Was it but vast unfathomed depths of water?

There was no death there, nor Immortality,
No Sun was there, dividing Day from Night.
Then was there only THAT, resting within Itself?
Apart from IT there was not anything.

At first within the Darkness, veiled in Darkness,
Chaos unknowable, the All lay hid,

Till straight away from formless void, made manifest
By the great Power of Heat, was born that germ.'
　　　　　　　Rig Veda XI, 29. Hymn of Creation

"Silence . . . mists . . . vapours, shadows, formless and
dark. A tremor and shudder—a vibrating crash . . . the
dancer, the dance and the melody fuse into the Eternal
Flame hiding within its white heat, the glow and the germ
of Life. The music pours in a torrent, it becomes the
rushing River of Life with its throbbing story of Birth,
Fulfilment and Death. Crimson and gold, life quickens
and pulsates. The elements leave . . . waters flow, petals
unfurl and far up in the Heavens shines a lone star . . .
iron-red. Fantasy, movement and colour, the dancer spins
into the beat and the rhythm of the moods. Ecstasy . . .
passion . . . enchantment . . . the smouldering movements
glow. Relentlessly the thin silver melody pierces in a
thousand different angles . . . pouring in livid streaks the
red flame of love and the white pain of life. A movement
ablaze with Light. Around the fire whirl the forces of life.
Elemental in their fury, unharnessed, unchecked, they
hurl themselves out from the bottomless depths. The
winds scream, the Waters crash in mighty waves. Leaping
and swirling, they spring into space, tearing the very
heavens down to their tempestuous bosom. The music
sweeps on up . . . up into a tornado of victory.

"All is calm, the storm has passed . . . the waters subside. The rhapsody in amber and gold fades away into the
dim velvety shadows. Silently the mists rise and vapours
melt. Far up in the sky the star is dead. On the river of
life no ripples caress the waters . . . no marks are left of
storms and tempests or Victory. LIFE IS ILLUSION . . .
LOVE . . . Fulfilment and Death . . . but a dream within a
dream.

"A sobbing flute pours out its melody . . its sweetness
lingers, rising and falling in rhythm with the heartbeats of
all time. Softly its haunting strain follows . . . sadly it
quivers as it dies away into a diminuendo of exquisite
tenderness . . . far, far away it flows to the edge of time
. . . to the ETERNAL SUNSET."

Who wrote these impressions? A lady in Colombo, Mrs.
Frieda Fernando.

Heinrich Zimmer, in his *Myths and Symbols in Indian Art and
Civilisation* expresses very clearly the image of Siva's dances.
As in all the main schools of Indian dancing there are pure
rhythmic and symbolic dances of Siva I feel that this great
Occidental scholar's observations simply convey the meaning
of Siva's sacred dances. Zimmer says:

"Dancing is an ancient form of magic. The dancer
becomes amplified into a being endowed with supra-
normal powers. His personality is transformed. Like
Yoga, the dance induces trance, ecstasy, the experience of
the Divine, the realisation of one's own secret nature, and
finally, mergence into the Divine essence. In India, consequently, the dance has flourished side by side with the
terrific austerities of the meditating grove-fasting, breathing exercises, absolute introversion. To work magic, to
put enchantments upon others, one has first to put enchantment on oneself. And this is effective as well by the
dance as by prayer, fasting and meditation. Siva, therefore, the Arch *Yogi* of the Gods, is necessarily also the
Master of the Dance.

"The dance is an act of creation. It brings about a new
situation and summons into the dancer a new and higher
personality. It has a cosmogenic function, in that it
arouses dormant energies which then may shape the world.

On a universal scale, Siva is the Cosmic Dancer; in his 'Dancing Manifestation' (Nritya-murti) he embodies in himself and simultaneously gives manifestation to eternal energy. The forces gathered and projected in his frantic, ever-enduring gyration, are the powers of the volition, maintenance and dissolution of the world. Nature and all its creatures are the effect of his eternal dance. Fire is the element of the destruction of the world. At the close of the 'Kali Yuga' fire will annihilate the body of creation, to be itself then quenched by the ocean of the void."

And so the Dance of Life moves on. All of life is effort and concentration and ideals achieved with no little difficulty.

I had felt this so strongly when I made a final tour of India in 1946–47. Restlessness was again upon me like a goad, compelling me to move on, to 'give' through the dance what I must to fulfil myself as an artist, as all artists must at some time or another. The dark lights had now lifted from the world, destruction was over and Mars, the War God, had retired to his spoils. This was Siva, life itself, for from that destruction a new order of life would come into being. There would be a new creation of life in the world. But somehow, beautiful as was the first spring after the war in India, my heart had known of death and loss and tragedy, and the fickleness of friendship and trust, and happy as I was, nothing could ever be the same. I was growing, all of life is growth, and the war had prematurely aged so much in the hearts of its living victims. All perhaps a process and pattern of God, in which Time alone would reveal the reasons of why and when and how?

India was moving into a new age, her age. The right to freedom Gandhi had proved at last, so that love could triumph over arms. He won his war with the spirit of love. The West had technically 'won' its war with arms, but sank deeper into further frustration and distrust, because her methods of 'winning' her wars, unlike those of Gandhi, had only set the chess-board of politics for further wars at some time to come, because her whole principle was wrong. Personally, I had won the love of that great public in my country by dancing and working for them through the medium of the Dance resurrected from a deep sleep of oblivion. But I had my enemies.

I heard so many stories about myself spread by rivals, even from some of the female pupils I had taken such pains to make into dancers. And then, too, there was a section of the public whom every artist finds is always ready to believe the worst. When all these 'stories' were repeated so often to me by my friends I would always remember the great words of the masters, the great philosophies of the *Gita*, that Song of God, and ignore them all. Every man of the theatre has enemies and friends. But is it really important what one's detractors say? Perhaps they can teach one many truths in their own way. After all, a few of the world's greatest masters and re-deemers from Lord Jesus Christ down to Gandhi, in our own time, have all had their full share and sacrifice at man's hands.

If I had to live my life all over again, I think I would still like to be a dancer and 'give' that beauty that overwhelms me when I dance. Up till now the Dance of Life, the theatre and beauty, have been my life-long purpose for living and working and learning and creating through the medium of my dance: not only a repetition of mere technique, devoid of 'inner realisation', but also to seek new avenues for using that technique in telling stories and dances and creating ballets that are something more than just a mere repetition of the past. Every creative artist has to contribute, recreating from old forms, new patterns, based on the old but living with the Truth of the present. That very same intensity of feeling for the Dance was what drove me then, so long ago as a little boy, and drives me, now, as a man, to "remind the whole world by my dance" of the truths hidden within the soul of man and revealed to him by the vision of beauty which I have glimpsed within my own soul.

India, Burma, Malaya, Java, China, the Phillipines and Japan and Hawaii, what a glorious memory the mention of those countries invokes within my mind. How much beauty and art was revealed to me by their temples, books and philosophies; and how I danced with all the fire and energy of my whole body to give them the best within myself through the dance.

"Giving is getting, my son"—said my mother. "Remember that when one dies, it's what one has given away in beauty and love that one takes with oneself, for these are incorruptible and eternal."

My tours of India and the Far East, enriched me beyond words in spirit and vision. And the East being one half of this world's circle, it was completed only when I toured so widely in England, America, France, Sweden, Denmark, Holland, Finaland and Norway, as also Switzerland and Turkey. Ireland has always held a special place in my heart, for it was Annie Besant, a spirited young woman from there, who taught India to be spiritually free.

Seasons of dance in London, New York, Paris. How filled with enriching experiences I was. Of course, what the public does not see are the hazards, untold physical fatigue involved in these world tours, and what the lack of finance can mean to an artist. From out front the picture has to be perfect. Indeed, it is only in the 'backstage' of life that the tremendous suffering and trials are seen by the few, misunderstood by the many, and sanctified by the 'elect', those wonderful friends who, because of their Belief in what one is trying to do, help unselfishly.

All my tours after the war in the great countries of the

West have only confirmed my belief that the role of the dancer is an even more vital and important one than ever before. For the Mirror of Gestures that an audience sees in the dance is a medium far more potent because of its visual appeal to the heart and mind of man. And it is there that the artist can make an appeal to man's highest nature, to turn from the darker instincts of war and hate, which seem to engulf and confuse so much of the world with a suspicion and evil that must inevitably bring destruction. In London, Paris and New York, and in all the great countries of this world, groups of dancers, visiting one another's countries from the East and the West, can do so much more than mere politicians who, try as they may, never seem to solve the problems of the world because of their ignorance of spiritual values and truth. If only they would read the old texts of God's chosen men on earth. If only . . . if only. . . . That is why it is in the Dance of Life, the Dance of Siva, that the world reflecting itself in a mirror, as it were, can, through the Dance, find one unerring medium of bringing about a universal sympathy and admiration, and that is a beginning. . . .

The soul of man is eternal, but to manifest the eternal principle, it has to keep reincarnating in a physical body. Christ, the divine spirit, said: "I come as the example for all men, and not an exception, which is often forgotten." But the soul of mankind has to learn its own lessons and so before each reincarnation it is given the earthly path it must take in order to continue its development.

There are no 'accidents' in life. How little this is understood when so constantly is heard 'if' one had done something, or 'if' something had happened. One has to use one's resources, naturally, but no man can prevent the hour when his soul is withdrawn from the earth or when it chooses to reincarnate. Christ said: "The Kingdom of Heaven is within" and those two great sages of India, Ramana Maharishi and Sri

Aurobindo, said the same thing. Then there is that wonderful statement Jesus made at the Last Supper: "I shall not drink again of the fruit of the Vine until I drink it anew with you in the Kingdom of Heaven."

The only true artist, whether in dance, drama, music, literature or painting, is the 'religious' artist, and in my dictionary it would mean the artist wholly dedicated to God's teaching, whether it comes from the East or the West. For it is then, and only then, that the artist transcends nationality and reminds the world of the immortality of beauty, which is Truth and God. Perhaps the great dance traditions of Japan, Bali, Java, Tibet and India have survived throughout the centuries, because they used a formalised technique for expressing the written truths of the great philosophers who wrote the 'Words of Commandments'. The great tradition of the ballet in Europe has yet to use its form for clothing old truths and expressing them in dance dramas.